A LARGER

FOR

MEMBERS OF

THE CHRISTIAN METHODIST
EPISCOPAL CHURCH

Expanded and Revised

by
Bishop Marshall Gilmore

Published by
The
CME Publishing House
Memphis, Tennessee
United States of America
William E. George, General Secretary

General Board of Publications
William E. George, General Secretary

ISBN: 1-883667-11-9

Library of Congress Catalogue
Card Number: 95-75186
Printed in the United States of America

TABLE OF CONTENTS

PreFace

The Larger Catechism is an endeavor to make available to the reading public in clear language information on Christian Methodist Episcopal (C.M.E.) doctrine, beliefs, polity and practices.

Those outside the C.M.E. Church may benefit from the book by using the information to become better informed and more conversant with it. Inter-denominational and ecumenical dialogue based on sound and solid biblical and theological information ought to enhance the spiritual well being of the body of Christ, or the Holy Catholic Church. Ignorance of denominations other than our own is without excuse in this information age.

Those who are members of the Christian Methodist Episcopal Church may benefit from the book in several ways. One, the information may be regarded to some extent as basic and primary. Introductory type information materials are part of the total body. Two, some of the doctrinal information will serve as growth material. Church members owe it to themselves to know the meaning of baptism and, more ever, how it is related to discipleship. The same may be said for the sacrament of Holy Communion. Three, Christian living expresses our truly Christian beliefs. Faithful members of the body of Christ desire to live all they know and understand above their faith. The increase of knowledge and understanding of the faith is the intentional design of this book.

I commend the Rev. William E. George, General Secretary of the Department of Publication for his conscientious commitment to the publication of good reading materials. I thank him for his personal encouragement and support for my writing ministry. And to the end that the people of God are blessed through it, to God be the glory.

Lent 1998

Marshall Gilmore

Chapter I

INTRODUCTION

A Personal Word

I have prepared this booklet, "A Catechism for Members of the Christian Methodist Episcopal Church," with the thought in mind of trying to begin the process of filling the need for handy information on Christianity and our church. It is not as tightly written, in terms of thought development, as I would like. However, I have tried to make it readable which I lose out on when I become too careful in writing. In spite of not being satisfied with it, I am presenting it because I believe its positive values outweigh its negatives.

What I cannot put on paper is my personal love for this church and the desire that I have to see our members develop a kindred spirit with its spirit of operations. We have a wonderful system, and we can make it great with some work. Get to know it and get a feel for it and sense how much potential it has for uplifting people and for glorifying God.

The references to the *Discipline* are to the 1986 Edition. Biblical references are generally to the Revised Standard Version.

"Joining the Church"

In this little section I want to discuss *how* we join the Church and *what* it means to join.

If an unbaptized individual comes forth when "the door of the Church is opened" the person is received as a "convert". A baptized member of another church may come forth to transfer membership by "Letter of Transfer" or by what we call "Christian Experience". The last means that the Pastor takes the word of the person who says that he or she belongs to a Church, in the Christian Way.

What about a youth or an adult who was baptized as an infant? First, a baptized infant is "in Christ" and in that important sense is a member of the body of Christ. Second, a baptized infant is in Christ by the graciousness of God and is the responsibility of the Church and the parents or sponsor for nurture, and teaching until the child is old enough to accept responsibility for self. Third, by joining the Church a youth or an adult baptized in infancy confirms his or her baptismal covenant (See C.M.E. *Book of Ritual*).

Those who join, for the most part, start as *Preparatory Members*, meaning they are preparing for full membership through instruction classes taught by the Pastor or his or her appointee. A second type of membership is *Associate* or *Affiliate*, which is for individuals living temporarily away from home and who desire pastoral oversight and the fellowship of a Church home while away.

Full Membership is the third type. For Preparatory Members this is the time when they are brought before the congregation, the Pastor having decided that the candidates are ready for full membership and the converts baptized, and given the opportunity to make known their commitment. Not only do those who are baptized at this time make a profession of faith in God through Christ, but as was pointed out earlier, those who were baptized in infancy and at other times, all of the new members are asked: "Will you be subject to the Discipline of the Christian Methodist Episcopal Church, and will you uphold the Christian Methodist Episcopal Church by your prayers, your presence, your gifts and your service?"

The question just quoted covers three aspects: (1) Our *voluntary promise* to be governed by the rules and regulations of the C.M.E. Church; (2) Our *voluntary promise* to attend church and to participate in the means of grace, and (3) Our *voluntary promise* to pay money, to use our time and our talents to support the Church.

The Christian Methodist Episcopal Church holds out one condition for Church membership. Which is a "desire to flee from the wrath to come, and to be saved from your sins." It maintains that "wherever this is really fixed in the soul, it will be shown by its fruits."

Each local Church exists to help us to grow in grace and to yield fruit. Three of its jobs which help us are (1) *Preaching Christ*, which is the Word of the Cross proclaimed as living and life giving power; (2) *Fellowship*, which is the visible mind and spirit of Christ. In other words, when the world sees the Local Church, it sees Christ, and (3) *Service*, which is the people of God being Christ in the world.

When we join a Church, we become a part of the body of Christ that is seen and known. By God's grace through faith we are in Christ which baptism makes known to those who are members already. With them by attending Church and taking part in the means of grace we work out our soul salvation in fear and trembling.

Using "the Catechism"

I suggest that leaders of groups where the Catechism is used to teach members that the sequence of chapters be followed. Which means that it should be used to teach a course consisting of several sessions.

This booklet is both a guide and a limited resource. So, the teacher will need a copy of the Holy Bible, and a copy of the latest C.M.E. *Book of Discipline*. In addition you will need a *History Of The C.M.E. Church* by Bishop O. H. Lakey and Bishop Joseph A. Johnson's book, *Basic*

Christian Methodists Beliefs and *The C.M.E. Primer* by Bishop C. D. Coleman. Surely, you will have the *Holy Bible* as your basic reference. May I suggest that you locate and read other books and pamphlets and booklets written by C.M.E.s. I have in mind such materials as *History of the C.M.E. Church* by Bishop Charles Henry Phillips, the autobiographical writings of Bishops B. Julian Smith, Henry C. Bunton and M. F. Jamison. Also, books have been written on the lives of Bishops Isaac Lane and L. H. Holsey that are informative. Finally, M. C. Pettigrew published *From Miles To Johnson* that you would do well to include in your C.M.E. Church background materials.

As I said in the outset of this discussion in presenting this material as a course, I suggest doing so by using one or two chapters for each session. As you go along questions may be asked to provoke discussion.

Acknowledgements

This edition of *A Catechism For Members Of The C.M.E. Church* was encouraged by the action of the General Conference in 1986 to make it the official training guide for new members. Bishop O. H. Lakey offered helpful suggestions for putting the material together, and I am grateful. The desire of Rev. L. L. Napier, General Secretary of the Department of Publications, to typeset the material and set it in book form prodded me into expanding it.

For the many years I have written articles and booklets and handouts, I am grateful to my wife, Yvonne, for abiding my preoccupation and the same is true of our offspring John Marshall and Joan Michele who somehow though at times impatient with my silence accepted my scribblings with wit and humor.

Ms. Debra Ann Kimble, my secretary, typed this manuscript as she did the *C.M.E. Discipline*, 1986, and *The Book of Ritual And Aids To Worship*. I owe her many thanks.

Marshall Gilmore
Advent 1987

Chapter II

FOUNDATIONS

ARTICLES OF RELIGION

1. **Do we have a standard or rule of doctrine to guide us in setting forth in writing, in teaching and in preaching our beliefs as a people of God?**

Yes. The Twenty-Five Articles of Religion that are printed in the *Discipline* constitute the standard and rule of doctrine of the Christian Methodist Episcopal Church.

2. **What is the background of the Articles of Religion?**

The Twenty-Five Articles of Religion are in part a shortened version of the Thirty-Nine Articles of the Church of England. John Wesley was not only a priest in the Church of England but also held that Church in great esteem. As a member he was at home with the 39 Articles of Religion.

"Generally, though not always, especially at first, Articles of Religion were distinguished from the Articles of the Faith. The latter were contained in the Creed. The former, while claimed to be accordant with and based upon the Creed, treated largely the contemporary questions in dispute."[1]

Luther, Melanchton and those who worked with them presented a body of Articles of Religion to the Germanic Diet at Augsburg, June 23, 1530 A.D., and is called the Augsburg Confession.[2] Several efforts were made by the Church of England to construct a body of Articles but due to several factors, such as, the failure to authorize Articles that had been drawn up as in the case of the English "Articles of Religion" of 1536, and the death of Henry VIII in 1547, which seemed to have slowed down the use of the Thirteen Articles of 1538.

The Thirty Nine Articles were set forth by the authority of the Queen, the Convocation and Parliament in 1571 A.D. They were made mandatory for subscription by a Canon of the Convocation and also by an enanctment of the civil legislature.[3]

The Methodist Episcopal Church in America was organized in 1784 in the Christmas Conference held at the Lovely Lane Church in Baltimore, Maryland. John Wesley, the priest in the Church of England, ordained Francis Asbury for the purpose of coming to the United States of America to serve as General Superintendent of the American Methodist Movement. It is a matter of history that Asbury refused to serve except he was elected by the preachers. They elected him and along with Dr. Thomas Coke they led the new church.

Since 1790 the Twenty Five Articles of Religion in their present form have been included in the *Disciplines* of American Methodism. The present form included Article Twenty Three (23) "Of the Rules of The United States of America" which was put in for the purpose of clearing away any doubt that might exist regarding the loyalty of Methodists to the civil government of the United States of America. With roots in English soil it was important to the Methodists that the air be cleared of any lingering suspicions.

3. **Can the Articles of Religion be changed?**

Let me begin by saying that the authority and power to change those things "connectional" in scope rest with the General Conference. It seems to me that the power to "regulate all matters relating to the form and mode of worship, ritual, and religious services and ceremonies subject to the limitations of the First Restrictive rule"[4] include, specifically, the Articles of Religion.

I hold that position because of the words of the First Restrictive Rule, which reads, thus.

> "The General Conference shall not revoke, alter, or change our Articles of Religion, or establish any standard or rule of doctrine contrary to our present existing and established standards of doctrine."[5]

The "full powers" principle related to the authority of the General Conference "to make rules and regulations for the Church" is limited. And Restrictive Rule One makes it clear that no matter at which end the amendment process starts, whether with the Annual Conferences or with the General Conference, there is a hedge or fence around the Articles that cannot be removed. The Articles of Religion are with us forever.

4. **Does the above position mean that the C.M.E. Church cannot adopt new doctrine?**

As I read it, Restrictive Rule One says two things. First, "the General Conference shall not revoke, alter, or change our Articles of Religion." So in a word, the legislative branch of our three part governmental system cannot enact into law "a rule of universal application" that revokes, alters, or changes *the body of material* that constitutes our "standard or rule of doctrine."

Second, the First Restrictive Rule prohibits the General Conference from *establishing* or ordaining or effecting "any *new* standards or rule of doctrine contrary to our present existing and established standards of doctrine.''

So, the General Conference cannot bother what is, that is, it cannot touch the Twenty Five Articles that we have, and neither can it bring into existence ''any new'' thing and set it up as the standards and rule of doctrine.

5. **Do the restrictions imposed by Restrictive Rule One on the General Conference keep us behind and make us outdated?**

I want to point out and do so now that basic religious doctrines should not and must not be set up so that they are open to changes that individuals and groups want to make at every General Conference. Each time the church gathers in legislative assembly we might find it necessary to say to some as the philosophers said to Paul in Athens, Greece, ''You bring some strange doctrines to our ears'' (Acts 17:20, paraphrased). Unlike Paul who stood on solid ground it is possible that some could rise up among us who have not yet attained ''to the unity of the faith and of the knowledge of the Son of God, to mature manhood, to the measure of the stature of the fulness of Christ'' (Eph. 4:13). Failing to have arrived at that level of maturity they are yet ''tossed to and fro and carried about with every wind of doctrine'' (Eph. 4:14). Being convinced of the rightness of the cunnings of men and crafty tongues where easy access to doctrine is available individuals may be tempted out of what they believe is good conscience to seek to revoke, change, or alter our established and present doctrine.

Basic doctrine is pretty well set, there may be new and novel ways of expressing and stating it. As long as new expressions do not violate the meaning they do not violate the standard or the rule.

When the Methodist Church and the Evangelical United Brethren Church united the issue was raised as to whether "the addition of the entire Confession of Faith of the E.U.B. Church constitute an "altering" of the Methodist Articles of Religion or the establishing of "new standards or rules of doctrine contrary to our present existing and established standards of doctrine."

Bishop Jack M. Tuell wrote that "Any examination of the two documents reveals that undoubtedly it does. For instance, Article XII of the E.U.B. Confession of Faith contain these words: 'We believe in the resurrection of the dead; the righteous to life eternal and the wicked to endless condemnation.' There is nothing in the articles which spells this out, particularly the last phrase concerning 'endless condemnation.' This, then, is the introduction of a new element into the Articles of Religion, which surely constitutes an altering of them."[6]

Bishop Tuell admitted that short of a new text being adopted a strong argument could be made to the effect that the Confession of Faith did not establish any "new standards or rules of doctrine *contrary* to our present existing and established standards of doctrine." "The two General Conferences in 1966 adopted the two doctrinal statements side by side, and adopted a resolution in which they 'deemed them congruent'."[7] Also, the Judicial Council of the United Methodist Church refused to get pulled into deciding the theological question regarding conflict between the Confession of Faith and the Articles of Religion. It left the matter up to the General Conference.[8]

The law of the C.M.E. Church states that "the Judicial Council shall exercise no jurisdiction over political, Theological, nor Doctrinal or civil affairs, ..."[9] So that if some effort was made to bring in new doctrine the General Conference would have to act on the matter.

No, I do not believe that the restrictions were intended to keep Methodism in the past. They protect it against the possibility of the theological foundations of the faith being destroyed. At the same time latitude exists for bringing new expressions to "old ideas." It seems to me there is a world of difference between a General Conference adopting an official standard of doctrine that is new and that of exercising its power to "regulate all matters relating to the form and mode of worship, ritual and religious services and ceremonies subject to the limitations of the First Restrictive Rule"[10] The latter law allows the General Conference to act affirmatively in such manner so as to bring into being documents, say the Social Creed, that may explicate official doctrine on the one hand and on the other hand translate the doctrine into practical theology, as it did by authorizing *The Book of Ritual.*

6. **So, there is room for creative thinking, and writing, and teaching and preaching without violating the Articles of Religion?**

By all means, there is adequate room for creative expressions. I think it is critical for the church that we not confuse doctrine with "rites and ceremonies" which "every particular Church may ordain, change, or abolish."[11] "Every particular Church" is not a reference to every local congregation. It refers to national churches and was meant to permit the

Church in each country to change rites and ceremonies "according to the diversity of countries." The Article herein quoted is applicable to the C.M.E. Church as an independent religious denomination subscribing to the Articles of Religion. But again this does not refer to doctrine as a body of material. Rites and ceremonies bring doctrine to life by using them in ritual and liturgy.

7. **What can a church member or a church do if it feels that it is being exposed by teaching or preaching to beliefs contrary to our official standard and rule of doctrine?**

The technical term for false teaching is heresy. It means "holding of a doctrine persistently contrary to the authoritative statement of it, a choice in error, and that a persistent choice."[12] The act of perverting the approved doctrine in our church is defined as "Disseminating and subscribing to doctrine contrary to the established standards of Doctrine of the Church."[13]

The "offense" is among those listed in the *Discipline* as "actionable," meaning that the accused is subject to a trial when charged with the offense.

THE GENERAL RULES

1. **Do we have a standard or rule for the practice of the Faith?**

Our rule or standard for the practice of the faith is the body of material known as the General Rules.[14]

John Wesley wrote the General Rules in 1743, May 1. They state, one, the requirement for admission to the Methodist Societies which is "a desire to flee from the wrath to come and to be saved from your sins,''[15] and, two, keeping them and repenting when they are not kept are the conditions for having a place within the Societies.[16]

According to Mr. Wesley we are taught of God to observe the General Rules, ''even in his written Word, which is the only rule, and sufficient rule, both of our faith and practice.''[17] The preceding statement must not go un-noticed. For it places both the Articles of Religion and the General Rules solidly upon the Holy Scriptures. It was a relationship that caused Wesley to be at odds with the Roman Catholic Church. He could not accept the fact that Rome did not recognize ''holy Scripture to be a sufficient rule for faith and manners'' but held instead that holy Scripture fell short according to ''many learned men'' of supplying grounds for some doctrines proposed by the Church as matters of faith, and some things required as necessary duty. The Roman Church added tradition to holy Scripture as the entire rule of faith. John Wesley denounced the decision to add tradition declaring it forbidden since God had not included it.[18]

2. **Are the General Rules also protected by the Restrictive Rules?**

Yes, they are protected by Restrictive Rule Four, which says, ''The General Conference shall not revoke or change the General Rules of the United Societies.''[19] However, the protection is not ultimate as in the case of the Articles of Religion. Under the Amendments provision of the Constitution of the C.M.E. Church Restrictive Rule Four can be amended.[20] Its amendment could conceivably lead to revoking or altering the General Rules.

3. **How can you make sense out of the General Rules?**

The General Rules are meaningful. They cover quite a range of behavior and when they are considered without contemporary bias or prejudice a wholesome prescription for life and living is discovered. They are divided into two parts. The first part is negative or passive, in the sense that it lists a group of things to be avoided.

Part two is positive or active in the sense that it contains a list of things to do that follows the words: "It is expected of all who continue in these societies, that they should continue to evidence their desire of salvation. Secondly, by doing good, by being, ... etc."[21]

4. **Are the General Rules binding upon the members of the C.M.E. Church?**

The question is interesting in that from a technical standpoint, that is, from the manner in which they are introduced, "The General Rules of the United Societies",[22] the question would seem to have legitimacy. Except, the Constitution of the C.M.E. Church made them our own and states that they "shall constitute the rules by which members of this Church shall strive to evidence their continual desire for salvation."[23]

And on that basis it is right and proper for the Presiding Elder to ask in Quarterly Conference "Have the General Rules been read?"[24] For what they contain constitute the rules by which we are to evidence our continual desire for salvation.

5. **Are we being hypocritical to hold to the General Rules as a standard but don't really keep them?**

The matter of hypocrisy is not limited to two-faced behavior regarding the General Rules. Hypocrite ''primarily denotes one who answers.'' Stage actors in Greece and Rome spoke in large masks with mechanical devices for increasing the volume of their voice. So the word became used metaphorically as a dissembler, a hypocrite.[25] A pretender might be another way to describe a hypocrite. Or the act of pretending to be what one is not by wearing a mask.

I suppose the question means that if the rule of the practice of faith for C.M.E.s is the General Rules, then, to have the rule and not follow it but behave otherwise is pretending. It is to behave as one who is hypocritical. Let me go back to the General Rules for guidance. By and large church members have problems with the first part of the General Rules. Which does not mean that they observe the positive part consisting of ''doing'' and ''being'' and ''attending.'' What troubles them are such things as ''avoiding'' ''drinking spiritous liquors;'' ''The putting on of gold and costly apparel'' and ''Laying up treasure upon earth''.

I call attention to two words which precede the negative list of things to be abstained or the evil to be avoided. The two words are ''such as''. Fredrick A. Norwood took those two words as the basis for removing a common meaning that is often given to the General Rules. Namely, they have ''sometime been misunderstood as setting rigid patterns of don'ts and do's.''[26] Once ''such as'' is given its proper place the General Rules are seen in a different light. ''the main content is simply examples of how holy living may find expression in daily life.''[27]

Norwood's viewpoint may be taken by some as the easier way out. Except, Wesley was not a legalist. To be a legalist a person has to cover every possible means and method whereby one might sin. We know that Israel had its religionists who had to make ''casuistic rules'' to make clear existing laws. For instance to hallow the Sabbath and keep it holy soon meant that what constituted work had to be defined so as to prevent people from doing what was not to be done as work on the Sabbath. One law not only begets many rules they become necessary to make the law practical and applicable to various situations.

The point is that to allow that Wesley drew up a list containing everything that was to be avoided in order to stay away from evil would be to go against the grain of a man for whom *doing* did not beget righteousness so much as believing did. To do was to fulfill the law of love. So believing that true Christianity is to love God wholly and to love the neighbor as one loves oneself Wesley regarded that the Christian is not a slave to law but to love. He wrote, saying, ''Never let the law of mercy and truth, of love of God and man, of lowliness, meekness, and purity, forsake thee.''[28]

The purpose of law in this manner is, one, for continually leading the believer to the atoning blood, continually leading to the confirmation of hope, ''till all the righteousness of the law is fulfilled in thee,'' and ''thou art filled with the fulness of God''.[29]

The law of sin is broken by the Spirit of God. ''Beware, then, thou who art called by the name of Christ, that thou come not short of the mark of the high calling. Beware thou rest not either in a natural state with too many that are accounted *good Christians*, or in a legal state, wherein those who are highly esteemed of men are generally content to live and die. Nay, but God hath prepared better things for thee, if thou follow on till thou attain. Thou art not called to fear and tremble like devils; but to rejoice and love, like the angels of God.''[30]

Whatever the view taken on the General Rules, strict or revisionist, you must conclude that they are purposeful. They were created out of the heart and mind of a man in response to a request in 1739 from eight or ten persons who came to London and asked John Wesley to meet with them. Out of that request and agreement the society was born which is no other than "a company of men having the form and seeking the power of godliness, united in order to pray together, to receive the word of exhortation, and to watch over one another in love, that they may help each other to work out their salvation."[31]

To assist in aiding seekers of godliness, to help them to help one another as they all worked, toward salvation and sanctification was part of the original purpose of the General Rules. And they can assist yet in that necessary undertaking. Sanctification or going on to perfection in love is still part of what is meant by being Christian.

THE SOCIAL CREED

1. **Do we have a document that provides us with positions on certain social, economic, and political issues?**

   Yes, the Social Creed of the C.M.E. Church[32] is the document. It was adopted by the General Conference in 1966, in Miami, Florida.

2. **Does a person have to read the whole document in order to get at something specific?**

   No. The Social Creed is divided into sections and subsections. Before I list the sections that deal with social issues I point to the fact that the Creed begins with a statement on "Our Heritage" which explains the basis of the concern of the C.M.E. Church for the social well-being of humanity. God's act of self revelation in Jesus of Nazareth and the life and witness of John Wesley are mentioned. Names of some leaders of our denomination follow.

Undergirding the sections is a "Theological Perspective" that sets forth our conviction that we are part of the body of Christ and this church "must express itself in the world in the light of the life and teachings of Jesus Christ." Following upon that statement are other affirmations which fill out the Perspective.

When the sections are considered they include "Economic Life" which consists of inflation, health services, wages and working conditions, automation, poverty and unemployment, urban life, and Christian vocation.

In terms of the church's responsibility we are "obligated to evaluate each aspect of the economic order by the commands of Christ and judge its practice by the Christian gospel."[33]

The second section deals with "the Church And General Welfare." Its sub-headings include peace and world order, the liquor problem, crime, gambling, sex and Christian life, and human rights.

Our churches are asked to do two things with the Creed. They are asked to study it and to put into practice the positions set forth in the various areas. From time to time local communities are faced critically with the problems and issues covered in our Social Creed, local churches should use it to address the issues and to act on them and use it to give our position as a denomination as necessary.

The Bible

1. **Do we have a foundation which undergirds and informs our standard of faith, which is the Articles of Religion, and our rule of practice, which is the General Rules, and our guide for social and economic ministries which is the Social Creed?**

   The Bible is the book that serves as the foundation for all of the above. John Wesley stated well the matter. He said, "In the year 1729, I began not only to read, but study, the Bible as the one, the only standard of truth, and the only model of pure religion."[34]

2. **Does this mean that we as Methodists do not use any other judge?**

   The fact that the Bible is the primary and supreme standard need not be interpreted to mean that we have to find proof texts to prove everything we say and do. Neither should it be interpreted to mean that we do not place other considerations in the process.

   Proof texting runs the risk of "making the Bible" mean something other than what the writer of a particular biblical book meant. After all the Bible tells the story of God's work of salvation. It centers in the self revelation of God which tells us who He is and who we are. In the story are certain major themes of which God's grace and human responses are dominant. The unfolding of His-Story presents us with ideas about God that may be translated by us into belief and action-oriented statements without having to back each of them with a Bible verse. The fact that God is constant and consistent makes the task easy and makes the result solid and compatible with His nature and behavior.

On the matter of other considerations, there is something known as the ''Wesleyan quadrilateral'' consisting of Scripture, tradition, experience, and reason.

John Wesley wrote that ''The Scripture ... is a rule sufficient in itself.''[35] However, he allowed that reason assisted by the Holy Ghost ''enables us to understand what the Holy Scriptures declare''.[36] The assistance He gives with ''the oracles of God'' which are the foundation as we can see is interpretive.

Truth was tested by reason and confirmed by experience. In other words without sacrificing the power of God and the miracle of faith the truth of Scripture should yield understanding which is what reason means in this context. *Experience* or life lived by faith confirms the truth that reason unfolds by the Holy Ghost. And beyond the experience that is personal or that an individual is able to confirm personally we have *tradition*, which is the content and the process of what is received out of the past, such as the experiences of individual Christians, and tradition is also the content and the process of experience passed on by us to generations following.[37] Examples for C.M.E.s would be the work of Bishop Isaac Lane on the mission fields in the Indian Territory or L. H. Holsey working to establish Paine College. Their labors were based on convictions grounded in faith. What they believed and achieved witness now to the truth of Scripture, of its testimony to faith. And their labors are worthy to be passed on to succeeding generations as evidence and witness to the truth of the Scriptures.

THE DISCIPLINE

1. **What is the *Discipline*?**

The Discipline of the Christian Methodist Episcopal Church is a book which contains, as of 1986, the foundations of the denomination, one as a member of the body of Christ, two, as a constitutional body, and three, as a legal entity, that is, a religious not for profit corporation authorized to be and to do within the United States of America. Further, it is a book that contains the administrative law and the trial law of this denomination.

Administrative law has to do with "technical processes and procedures" of the C.M.E. Church. It deals with polity or church government and church practices or how the polity is to be carried out. Trial law has to do with the trial of ordained ministers; of lay members, with the appeal process, and with the whole process of Judicial Administration.

Going back to the above reference to 1986, prior to the General Conference held that year each complete book of *Discipline* contained our ritual and orders of worship. In 1986 the General Conference authorized the printing of a separate *Book of Ritual*.

2. **How long have we had a book of *Discipline*?**

We, the C.M.E. Church, adopted the *Book of Discipline* of the Methodist Episcopal Church, South in 1870, "making only such verbal alterations and changes as may be necessary to conform it to our name and the peculiarities of our condition."[38]

The *Book of Discipline* in American Methodism originated in 1785 and by 1792 what had been a "rather simple and unorganized" book was "reorganized into three chapters: ministry, membership, and temporal economy.'' Due to the schism caused by James O'Kelly whose motion was defeated that asked the General Conference of November 1792 to give preachers appointed by the bishop in conference the right of appeal if they thought themselves injured by the appointment, ''the General Conference of 1796 instructed the bishops to prepare explanatory notes replete with fortifying scripture passages for the *Discipline*. This was incorporated in the edition of 1798.''[39]

3. **What is the authority for discipline?**

Jesus gave a disciplinary procedure to his disciples for a brother who sinned against any one of them (Matt. 18:15-20).

There are those who have argued that necessity is the authority for discipline. The argument runs, thus: ''A discipline is necessary to the very existence of Church organization. The Church has the right, therefore, to make, enforce, and construe its own discipline. It is as much a delusion to confer religious liberty, without the right to make and enforce rules and regulations, as it is to establish and maintain a government with no power to punish offenders.''[40]

4. **What is the purpose of discipline?**

The portion known as administrative law exists for the orderly working of the institution that the mission of the church may be realized and fulfilled through its several and diverse ministries. If this statement is put beside our conference structure, and the organizations within the conference at each level with an eye to conferences and organizations as PEOPLE and not as print on a paper the words of Ephesians 4:16 ''when each part is working properly'' leap out at you. Discipline is designed, therefore, to facilitate the proper and orderly working of "each part."

Trial law exists "to clear the innocent, to rebuke offenders, to reclaim the erring, to remove scandals, and vindicate the character of the church, to promote purity and peace in the membership, and for the spiritual welfare of the offenders themselves."[41] So in the final analysis trial law is basically redemptive and is not designed primarily to be punitive.

METHODISM

1. **Since we are Methodists what is the history of Methodism?**

For some persons Methodism had its beginning May 24, 1738. It was on that date that John Wesley, the Father of Methodism, had an experience of which he wrote, saying:

> "In the evening I went very unwillingly to a society in Alders-gate Street, where one was reading Luther's preface to the Epistle to the Romans. About a quarter before nine, while he was describing the change which God works in the heart through faith in Christ, I felt my heart strangely warmed. I felt I did trust in Christ. Christ alone for salvation. And an assurance was given me, that he had taken away *my* sins, even *mine*, and save *me* from the law of sin and death."[42]

Bishop Gerald Kennedy wrote of John Wesley regarding May 24, 1738 that it "was nothing less than a turning point in his life and the spring of the Methodist flood."[43]

2. **What, then, is John Wesley's background?**

John Benjamin Wesley was born June 17, 1703, Epworth, England. His parents were Samuel, a priest in the Church of England, and Susanna Wesley. They were parents of nineteen (19) children and John was the fifteenth (15th).

John was educated at Oxford University. His undergraduate work was in Christ Church, which was part of Oxford. At the age of 22 years he was ordained Deacon in Christ Cathedral, and was ordained a priest in 1728 in the same place. In 1727 he received the M.A. degree from Oxford with special emphases in the classics and theology.[44]

John Wesley was an Anglican priest who began a ministry to "the common people." Soon he was denied access to his own churches, that is, congregations of the Church of England. When denied he preached in the open fields and wrote of it, "I preached to a huge multitude in Moorfields on, Why will ye die, O house of Israel? It is the field preaching which does the execution still; for its usefulness there is none comparable to it."[45]

He did not set out to start a new church. But his activities disturbed the Church of England so he found himself an outsider. He was compelled almost to organize the abundant supply of the fruits of his labors. In 1739 he organized his first Methodist Society and did so in London, the city of his heart-warming experience.

3. **How did Methodism cross the Atlantic Ocean to the new world, of North America?**

Possibly, there ought to be a distinction made between the "un-official" and the "official" bearers of Methodism across the ocean. Let us note that

Wesley held his first Conference in 1744 which gave some structure and beginning to Methodism as an organization.

The first or the ''earliest planters'' of Methodism in America ''were certainly un-authorized.'' Wesley learned of them when they sought help from him in 1768. Maryland was probably the scene of the first plantings but evidence shows that a society was in New York from 1766, the one in Maryland was begun about six months earlier. Robert Strawbridge an Irishman, was the key figure in Maryland. He was a layman who took up preaching on his own. In New York Barbara Heck, a lay woman, led the way with Philip Embury. From their labors in organizing a society John Street Methodist Episcopal Church would be organized later.

The official and authorized planters of Methodism were men such as Richard Boardman and Joseph Pilmore who arrived in Philadelphia, October 22, 1766. In 1771 Francis Asbury and Richard Wright arrived. Thomas Rankin and George Shadford came in 1773.[46]

Francis Asbury and Thomas Coke are the two representatives whose names and work may be best known.

4. **When was Methodism officially organized in America?**

It was organized in ''the Christmas Conference'' of 1784 in the Lovely Lane Meeting House, Baltimore, Maryland. The first name was the Methodist Episcopal Church in America.

5. **Who were its earliest leaders?**

Francis Asbury and Thomas Coke were the earliest elected leaders. John Wesley set Coke apart to be a ''general superintendent'' of the American Methodists. But something unique happened when the Christmas Conference acted on December 24, 1784. Asbury wrote, that, ''When the conference was seated, Dr. Coke and myself were unanimously *elected to the superintendency* of the Church, ...'' For the first time in Methodism all things were determined by a majority of votes. The Conference concept was born.[47]

6. **With one Methodist church in 1784, when did all of the others come about?**

A series of schisms, splits, and divisions have occurred in Methodism in America. Elsewhere I noted some of them but I will go to the James O'Kelly fracture of 1792 over the authority of bishops to have full power to appoint preachers. O'Kelly tried but failed to have that changed to where a preacher who was not satisfied with the assignment could appeal to the Annual Conference and if upheld get a new charge. He and others left and formed the short-lived Republican Methodist Church, which became later the Christian Church.[48]

In 1830 the Methodist Protestant Church was organized over dissatisfaction with the unlimited powers of the episcopacy and the lack of laymen in the Annual and General Conferences. The Wesleyan Methodist Church was organized in May of 1843, at Utica, New York. Its members did not want slaveholders as members and they had lay representation in their church.

The Free Methodists left the Church in 1860. In 1894 eight small holiness groups who had left Methodism united to form the Church of the Nazarene.[49]

In 1844 there was a major division which gave birth to the Methodist Episcopal Church, South. The Methodist Episcopal Church continued. The C.M.E. Church came out of the M.E. Church, South.

7. **Where did the Black Methodist churches come from?**

The African Methodist Episcopal Church and the African Methodist Episcopal Zion Church are both out of the Methodist Episcopal Church.

The members who started the A.M.E. Church came out of the St. George Methodist Episcopal Church in Philadelphia, Pennyslvania in protest over the treatment of blacks in 1787. The church was organized first as Bethel Church under the leadership of Richard Allen. He also organized the ''Free African Society'' instead of an independent church. But after the M.E. Church would not ordain him Elder he moved to form a ''Christian Confederation'' around 1813 consisting of several churches of the Free African Society. In April of 1816 the A.M.E. Church was organized in Philadelphia. Richard Allen became its first bishop.[50]

The A.M.E. Zion Church according to Bishop William J. Walls was founded October 1796 in New York City. Its members withdrew from the John Street M.E. Church. But it was not until July 26, 1820 that its members voted themselves out of the Methodist Episcopal Church. James Varick was the leader of this group. After great efforts at trying to get regular ordination for their preachers, Abraham Thompson, James Varick and Leven Smith were ordained elders by ''three regularly ordained Methodist elders'' on Monday night, June 17, 1822.

Varick was elected first Superintendent and consecrated July 30, 1822.[51] The term ''Zion'' was added to the name of the church in 1848. It also changed the title of its spiritual leaders from Superintendents to Bishops.

A third black church was the African Union Church. It was Methodist in polity. The churches called their pastors. Their bishops were referred to as presidents. Its history goes back to 1805, Wilmington, Delaware was its center and Peter Spencer was its leader.[52]

8. **Have any of these churches re-united?**

The black Methodists are still independent organizations. A major union took place in 1939 between the M.E. Church, the M.E. Church, South, and the Methodist Protestant Church, which resulted in the organization of the Methodist Church.

Then in 1968 the Methodist Church and the Evangelical United Brethren Church united to form the United Methodist Church.

Chapter III

BASIC BELIEFS-A

THE HOLY TRINITY

1. **What do we mean by the Trinity?**

Let me say that we do not mean by the Trinity that there are *three Gods*. We do mean that there is *one God* of three persons in the Godhead.

I do not want to cop out but I must say that the Trinity is an effort to express mystery. And when all is said and written on the subject of the Trinity, the mystery will remain. In plain talk the Trinity is the church's effort to teach that which it understands in part. That is, the Trinity is about the mystery as to how God the Creator became human in Jesus of Nazareth, the Redeemer, and is now God the Holy Spirit, the Sustainer. What we must keep in mind is that while there are many ways of expressing the meaning of the Trinity all of them do not safeguard God's one-ness nor His unity. The unity of God is important to our keeping faith with the Bible.

The words of Deuteronomy may be used as an illustration of the biblical concept of one-ness. The words are "Hear, 0 Israel; the Lord our God is one Lord" (Deut. 6:4). Holding the unity of God intact is important for unity expresses the truth that God is neither divisible nor is He many. He is the *one-ly*.

2. **How may we best go about understanding what is meant by the Trinity?**

There have been at least two approaches to dealing with the Trinity. One approach has taken the route of the so-called *Trinity of Transcendence*. It attempts to describe or discuss God in communion *with* Himself (I John 5:7). God-In-Himself is Father, Son (John 8:41) and Spirit (Gen. 1:2).

The second approach is the *Trinity of Experience* which may mean that God-In-Himself is the same as He is experienced in history. The God revealed to us as Redeemer (Rom. 3:21-26) is none other than the Creator (Isa. 40:20) who is also the contemporary Sustainer and Keeper and Companion (John 14:15-17; I Thess. 4:8).

3. **What does the Trinity deal with?**

What the Trinity deals with is *one God, three persons*. During theological seminary days I was told that person in this way meant the mask worn by actors on the Greek stage, which made it possible for the same actor to play several different parts simply by changing masks. So there was one actor in three persons. When the idea is used to express God revealed there is one God in three persons, Father, Son and Holy Ghost.

The three persons of the Godhead are God completely and fully. Conversely, God who reveals Himself as Father, Son and Holy Spirit is in each revelation one and He is there fully and completely.

We may say that God the Father creates; God the Son redeems, and God the Holy Spirit sustains. But we must not allow ourselves to slip into thinking that God is less or more in one or the other of His activities. He is eternally and totally and completely and wholly God in each.[1]

4. **What do we believe about God?**

We believe that there is one God (Gal. 3:20); living and true (I Thess. 1:9-10), uncreated, eternal and everlasting (Isa. 40:28; Rom. 16-26); all-powerful (Gen. 17:1, II Cor. 6:14-18), and perfect (Matt. 5:48);

unlimited in love and mercy (I Chron. 16:34, Pss. 23:6, 136:1); the Creator of heaven and earth and all who dwell therein (Gen. 1:1, Mal. 2:10, Eph. 3:9, Col. 1:16, Rev. 4:11).

God is the Liberator of the oppressed from bondages one and all (Exod. 3:7-12, Lk. 4:16-21).

From the basics just stated we may expand in many directions. But the most helpful may be that of saying something about a particular statement that is recorded in the Bible. The statement is this: "God is love" (I John 4:16b).

"God is love" is a belief that flavors and tempers His eternal being, His power and perfection, His limitless love and His boundless mercy; and gives meaning to His creative accomplishments.

Love is an emotion and an action that demands and requires relationships. Love needs an object towards which it is directed. The object may be self and when love is directed towards self it really loses its right to be called love. Essentially love reaches out and that is precisely what the Bible says, "For God so loved the world that he gave his only begotten Son, that whosoever believeth in him should not perish, but have everlasting life" (John 3:16).

Love is redemptive (Rom. 5:8) and relational (John 4:23) and the God who is Spirit (John 4:20) reached out in Jesus of Nazareth to establish a relationship with the whole of creation (Rom. 8:21-23). In reaching out God made it possible for us to love (I John 4:10-11). The love that we have from God we share with Him by loving one another (I John 4:16, 20, 21). And the love of God that we have as dwellers in Him (I John 4:13) which dwelling is attested to by the gift of His Spirit to us (I John 4:13b) is love both for living and for dying. Love is indeed the seal of

His guarantee that nothing shall be able to separate us from Christ (Rom. 8:35a). That which we cannot be separated from in this life and in the world to come is the love of Christ. Forever the people who belong to God who is love and Spirit participate and share in His life both here and "there," for when we move from here to there "the dust shall return to the earth as it was ... and the spirit shall return unto the God who gave it" (Eccl. 12:7).

God is all powerful, all knowing all everywhere but this God who is Spirit is eminently LOVE.

5. **What do we believe about Jesus?**

We believe that Jesus is the Son of God (Matt. 3:17, Matt 1:18-25). He was born of the virgin Mary (Luke 2:1-7). He lived a life of ministry under the control and guidance of God's Spirit (Luke 4:16-27). He suffered under Pontius Pilate (Luke 23:1-25). On Friday he was crucified (Matt 27:35ff.), until he was dead (Matt. 27:50, Mark 15:37; Luke 23:46b). He was buried in a tomb of Joseph of Arimathea (Matt. 27:57-60). He was raised by God from the dead (Rom. 10:9; Gal. 1:1) on Sunday—the third day (Acts 10:40). He was seen by many men and women after His resurrection (I Cor. 15:1-8). Forty days after God raised Jesus of Nazareth the Christ of God (Matt. 16:16) he ascended into heaven (Acts 1:9). From there he will come again to judge the living and the dead (I Pet. 4:5, II Timothy 4:1).

In the context of all that is written above, let me say that we believe that Jesus "became a human being" (Heb. 2:14, Phillips) and took on death, the last enemy of God (I Cor. 15:26) and prevailed as victor over death and the grave (I Cor. 15:55). Not only did Jesus reveal God to us (John 14:8, 9), He revealed us to ourselves (Philp. 2:1-11).

Jesus of Nazareth (Luke 4:22) the Son of man (Matt. 16:13) was indeed very God (John 10:30) and very "human being" (Heb. 2:14). In him love was revealed without blemish, spot or wrinkle but in its purity and its beauty.

Jesus love perfect in being and doing was one with the Father in will (John 6:38-40) and in work (John 4:34, 9:4, 17:4).

6. **What is our belief in the Holy Ghost?**

We believe the Holy Ghost is the third person of the Godhead. He is the gift of the Father and the Son (John 14:26, 15:26). He is "the Lord, the life giver" (II Cor. 3:17, John 6:63). He is worshipped and glorified with the Father and the Son. He is Companion and Comforter.

7. **What is meant by the baptism of the Spirit?**

John the Baptizer who baptized with water promised that one who would come after him "shall baptize you with the Holy Ghost, and with fire" (Matt. 3:11b). Just before his ascension Jesus told his disciples "before many days you shall be baptized with the Holy Spirit" (Acts 1:5).

In an effort to say what is meant by "the baptism of the Spirit" let me point out that there are at least two different views on whether the work of Spirit in regeneration or the new birth is one with baptism of the Spirit. One view holds that the Spirit at work in the new birth of individuals (John 3:6, John 1:13, Rom. 5:5, Gal. 3:1-5, Eph. 2:13-18, I John 4:2) is effected together with the baptism of the Spirit. In other words, when a person is born again which is the work of the Holy Spirit that work is also the baptism of the Spirit.

The Second view holds that baptism of the Spirit comes *after* regeneration and not *with* it. Major support for this position is found by appealing to the question that Paul asked some disciples at Ephesus. He asked, "Did you receive the Holy Spirit *when* you believed?" (Emphasis mine). They answered him, saying, "No, we have never heard that there is a Holy Spirit." These disciples had been baptized in John's baptism. So they were baptized in the name of the Lord Jesus. Then, Paul laid his hands upon them and "the Holy Spirit came on them; and they spoke with tongues and prophesied" (See Acts 19:1-7).

8. **Does the coming of the Holy Spirit upon the disciples after they believed mean that such is always the case?**

No. For the reason that John's disciples fell into a special group. It is not likely that news of Pentecost had reached Ephesus. Their ignorance, "we have never heard that there is a Holy Spirit," was not an indictment on anyone. They stated a fact based upon the failure of news to reach them where they were.

J. Oswald Sanders maintained that there are two other groups in the same class with the disciples at Ephesus. The unique character is that for a reason the speaking in tongues was part of the coming of the Spirit upon the people. However, it must be understood from biblical practice that the three groups were each special and should not be taken as examples of Divine policy and practice that He carried out universally in every particular situation. Nor should the speaking in tongues be expected as though it was a possible human experience that God has promised to every believer.[3]

From the record the two other groups are the company waiting in the Upper Room in Jerusalem for the coming of the Holy Spirit (Acts 1:5-7), and the group at Caesarea. The former group here was given tongues to prepare it for Peter's preaching and the latter or third group received tongues to show the unbiased nature of God despite Peter's prejudice (Acts 10).

9. **Will you say a few words on "Speaking with tongues"?**

Before tongue speaking is exalted two things need to be said. First, the amazement of the people was due to their understanding of what was said though every person spoke in his or her own language. No matter that they represented many different geographical regions they said, "we hear them telling in our own tongues the mighty works of God" (Acts 2:11). Second, the three thousand converts resulting from the sermon preached by Peter were converted as *he spoke in his own tongue* and not in other tongues (Acts 2:14ff).

John Wesley in his preaching took great pain to show that what happened on Pentecost did not happen, for instance, when the church prayed later. That is, the place of assembly shook, the people were filled with the Holy Ghost but their speaking of the word of God was with boldness (Acts 4:31). As Wesley noted the *extra-ordinary gifts* are not mentioned. He concludes that the emphasis should be on *ordinary fruit* (See I Cor. 12:9, 10, 12:28-30; Gal. 5:22-24).[4]

10. **When does baptism of the Spirit come, if at all?**

Baptism in the Holy Spirit is an initiatory act, it is the process of induction into the church of Jesus the Christ. Paul wrote saying, "For by one Spirit we were all baptized into one body—Jews or Greeks, slaves or free—and all were made to drink of one Spirit" (I Cor. 12:13).

J. Oswald Sanders took the above quoted verse and made the following observations. (1) The baptism of the Spirit is common to *all believers*; (2) It is a *past event* in the believer's life, (3) It refers to the believer being *incorporated into the body of Christ*, and (4) There is no *distinction among believers* in this respect.

When we accept Christ as the Savior and Lord of our lives and are baptized in the name of the Father, Son, and Holy Spirit we partake in the baptism of the Spirit. The baptism of the Holy Spirit took place on the day of Pentecost and we are heirs to His presence. Once we receive him by virtue of receiving Christ through faith we must desire to "Be filled with the Spirit" (Eph. 5:18), which means being Spirit possessed and voluntarily and completely controlled by God.

11. **Should we tarry and wait to be filled?**

Tarrying did not bring the Holy Spirit to the Upper Room in Jerusalem on Pentecost. The atmosphere and the climate created by a people who "with one accord devoted themselves to prayer" (Acts 1:14), cultivated their minds and put their spirits in tune with their obedient bodies that assembled to await the fulfillment of the promise of Jesus. But "the filling" took place by virtue of the sovereign will of God.

We do not need to tarry just to be filled with the Spirit. What a shame that tarrying has been reduced to a time of waiting for the gifts of tongues, and some individuals would have us believe except we speak in tongues we are not saved because we do not have the Spirit.

Remember the Trinity? Do you recall that God is one? which means not only that He is *not divided* but it means also that He is *not divisible*. Did I not state that the three persons are of the one God? So, if one does not have the Spirit that individual does not know God. Speaking in tongues is not what that person needs. Being born again is. When that happens the Spirit is given.

The Spirit is unavoidable for being saved, he is prominent in the work of redemption. John's First Epistle speaks of *knowing* that we abide in God and God in us. He said we know that is happening "because he has given us his own Spirit" (I John 4:13). The abiding involves critically confessing "that Jesus is the son of God" (I John 4:15). But "no one can say 'Jesus is Lord' except by the Holy Spirit" (I Cor. 12:3) which says if there is a sequence in salvation that indeed "the Spirit helps us in our weakness" (Rom. 8:26). He is before our being saved for it is by putting to death the deeds of the body by the Spirit that we live (Rom. 8:13b). By God's Spirit life is His gift to us "through his Spirit which dwells in" us (Rom. 8:11b). Let it go out from the Christian Methodist Episcopal Church that "anyone who does not have the Spirit of Christ does not belong to him" (Rom. 8:9).

It seems to me that tarrying for receiving the Holy Spirit is futile, since he is given by God for our believing and he becomes a resident in us (Rom. 8:9; I Cor. 3:16, 6:19; 12:3; II Cor. 6:16).

Likewise with tarrying for the Holy Ghost so as to speak in tongues, which is but one gift of the Spirit and an inferior one at that (I Cor. 14:4-32). We should not expect everyone to have the same spiritual gifts. The gifts are not inherited neither are they acquired by human efforts. Rather, "All ... are inspired by one and the same Spirit who apportions to each one individually as he wills" (I Cor. 12:11, Also, see I Cor. 12:1-31).

12. **Is there a difference between the *gift* of the Spirit and the *gifts* of the Spirit?**

Yes. The gift of the Spirit was what God gave to the Church on the day of Pentecost. The Spirit is for every member of the body of Christ, the church.

On the other hand, the gifts of the Spirit (I Cor. 12:4ff) are special and are bestowed upon each individual according to God's plan and purpose for the individual. The gift of the Spirit is for always. The gifts of the Spirit if not used may not be revoked nor recalled (Rom. 11:29) but the possessor by sin may indeed affect their usefulness (I Tim. 4:14-16).

13. **Do the gifts of the Spirit serve any useful purpose?**

That question really borders on being an insult to God who does not deal in idle or purposeless things. To be sure the gifts are given for service. In fact, Paul wrote that persons are given "the manifestation of the Spirit for the common good" (I Cor. 12:7). The gifts of the Spirit are diverse but all of them are directed towards one point, "the common good." And the common body in which the common good is to be done is the church. Paul also said, "since you are eager for manifestations of the Spirit, strive to excel in building up the church" (I Cor. 14:12).

14. **Will you kind of pull together what you have been saying?**

I have tried to say that the Holy Spirit is God. He is not a lesser God than the Father and the Son. He came from the Father upon the request of the Son (John 14:15-17). Jesus was in the world in the form of a physical material body. His peculiar office was the Messiah, the Anointed of God and he served his office as a Suffering Servant who died for the sins of many.

The work of the office of the Holy Spirit is life giving. He quickens or brings to life that which is dead to life. He is therefore creative, bringing new life out of what was dead. He comforts and strengthens and behaves mysteriously (John 3:5-8) but he is never disorderly. "For God is not a God of confusion but of peace" (I Cor. 14:32). What he does he does "for edification" (I Cor. 14:26c) of the church, the body of Christ. Thus, the gifts that he gives to individual believers are to be used so as to benefit all and not for selfish advantages nor are they to be used in boasting of one's superior righteousness and of the inferior spiritual state of another sister or brother in Christ.

The Holy Spirit baptizes one into the one body of Christ, the church, and from the beginning of the new birth he is in the believer. Our responsibility is to grow in grace so that he who is in us might also completely and totally possess us.

THE HOLY SCRIPTURES

1. **What is the Bible?**

The English word "Bible" comes from a Greek word (ta biblia) which means "The Books." That makes a lot of sense since as we know the Bible that we use consists of sixty-six (66) books.[5]

The Bible is, then, a collection of books. A kind of library under one cover, so to speak.

But the Bible is more than a collection of books under the same cover. George Potts wrote that "The word Bible simply means "Book".[6] Yet that does not get to the words written on the front part of the cover of the Book, namely "Holy Bible."

The word "Holy" means separated or set apart. Holy distinguishes the Bible as a Book from any other book. The Bible is a Holy Book because of Him whose story it tells. God uses the words that He breathed into human beings as vessels to reveal Himself.

So the Bible is the written account of God's creative, God's seeking, God's saving and sustaining activity in human history. The Bible is the Word of God telling of His self revelation "in order to be known". In His revelation the written record shows that "He chose a certain group of people—the Jewish nation, the patriarchs and prophets and apostles as His witnesses; all these witnesses point in the same direction, they witness to the coming of Christ as the One Revealer and Redeemer" of humankind.[7]

The Bible is the written record of Jesus of Nazareth, the Christ of God, his ministry as expressed in his birth, life, death, resurrection and ascension. It is the written story of the church bought by the blood of Jesus (Acts 20:28) and of its faith and its hope kept alive by its worship and witness between the times of Christ's departure and his return in the end-time in power and glory to receive the church unto himself.

2. **How does the Bible, the Book, become the Word of God for an individual?**

The Bible becomes the Word of God for the believer as the Holy Ghost reveals God in His Christ through the written words (Matt. 16:17, I Cor. 2:6-10, 12:3). The letters on the written pages remain just a bunch of alphabets tied together until the Spirit, the Life Giver, lifts them off with the impress of God stamped upon them and touches our lips with them and lays them upon our hearts.

3. **Does faith play a part in the process?**

Faith is important in hearing the Word of God in human words. But the mystery is in the fact that the faith with which we hear God is also created by the very same Word that we hear (Rom. 10:17). Here again the Spirit is at work. The sword of the Spirit is the word of God (Eph. 6:17). By its own capacity the Word which is "living and active and sharper than any two-edged sword" (Heb. 4:12) cuts away spiritual debris so that any of us may respond to the words of Jesus who said, "He who has ears to hear let him hear" (Matt. 11:15). So, the Spirit of God brings about the revealing of the Word of God in everyday kinds of human words. How it happens is a mystery. Yet anyone who has read the Bible prayerfully and carefully meditating upon its words knows that again and again a light comes on suddenly. And what had been nothing more than mere words takes on meaning and provides a window for peeking into the ways of God. Internally, there is illumination as "the surprise of joy" is experienced. And we know that the letter by the Spirit lives. The letter is made alive and is life offering.

4. **What is the meaning of "the sufficiency of Holy Scriptures"?**

The form of the above question may take that of the one asked by the Minister to a person being received into the church. Namely, "Do you receive and profess the Christian faith as contained in the Scriptures of the Old and New Testaments?" That form used in this way shows not only belief but action based on belief. The believer receives and professes the sufficiency or power of the Christian faith to save.

Another form of the question and one that is close kin to the above is part of our ritual used in the ordination of the Elder in the C.M.E. Church. The Bishop asks: "Are you persuaded that the Holy Scriptures contain all truth required for eternal salvation through faith in Jesus Christ?"

The last question brings out the role of faith in salvation. So what Article of Religion Five means is that yes the Holy Scriptures do contain everything that we need to know in order to be saved. And what they contain is the story of God who offered His only Son to save the world. And His Son finished the work of redemption (John 19:30), a work of benefits on behalf of the whole world, on behalf of all humanity and in behalf of all history. Until the end of time His grace is there for faith to receive unto personal salvation (Eph. 2:8-9).

The Scriptures tell the story of salvation history and they tell the story of how individuals may become part of the history.

5. **What is our belief about the Old Testament?**

We believe that the Old Testament is not contrary to the New. Because in both, everlasting life is offered in Christ.

Let me insert here that "Christ" is used by Christians as though the term refers to Jesus' last name. When in fact "Christ" is a title and means the Messiah or the Anointed One. When Peter answered Jesus' question, "Who do you say that I am?," with the words "You are the Christ, the Son of the living God" (Matt. 16:16), he was commended for the answer which revealed of God declared Jesus of Nazareth to be the Christ.

I do not wish to oversimplify nor understate the matter but to understand Christ from the side of the Old Testament means looking for and expecting "someone" to be elected by God to the office of Messiah. And when we speak of Jesus of Nazareth as the Christ it is always a matter of doing so *by faith*. Of course "the Jesus kick" that seems to have an emotional hold on so many Christian individuals avoids the question of faith or belief in Jesus as the Christ. Which falls short of coming to grips with what was indeed a very important issue during the ministry of Jesus as was revealed in his questions to his disciples (Matt. 16:13-20).

Back to the matter of over-simplifying: In the Old Testament the Messiah is *expected* and in the New Testament and the Church the Messiah is *believed* to have come in Jesus of Nazareth.

I have noticed that we have accepted the words "the Christian faith as contained in the Old and New Testaments" when they are put to us in questions on church membership and on orders. The easy acceptance (I suppose) indicates, at least, that either we are at home with them or the issues are not important.

6. **Are all parts of the Old Testament binding upon Christians?**

No. All parts of the Old Testaments are not binding upon Christians, especially those that deal with ceremonies and rites. Also, the civil precepts of the Old Testament should not be looked upon by any Commonwealth as mandatory as civil laws. Christians are bound by its moral laws.[8]

Many of the ceremonies and rites and civil laws are found in the biblical books of Leviticus and Numbers. The moral laws are given in Exodus 20 and to some extent they are rehearsed in Deuteronomy 5-11.

7. **How many books are in the Bible?**

We subscribe to sixty-six (66) books as the canonical books of the Holy Bible.

Thirty-nine (39) books make up the Old Testament and the New consists of twenty-seven (27).

It took approximately one thousand years to write the Bible. The time span was from about 850 B.C. to about 100 A.D.

8. **Does your answer imply there are other Bibles with more or less books in them?**

Yes. I had in mind the fact that there are Bibles with more books in them than are in the one we accept as canonical.

First, let us get the word "canon" in hand. It means measuring rod or a standard of measurement. So the sixty-six (66) books in "our Bible" measure up to the standard set for inclusion by the Church.

Second, there is a group of books called "the Apocrypha" (hidden) which are included in Pulpit Bibles but are not accepted as canonical. The Responsive Readings in some hymnals use materials from these books. The references may be missed because names of a book such as Eccles**tiacus** is so much like our Eccles**tiastes** (Emphasis mine). Third, the Bible used by the Roman Catholic Church included more books than our own.

9. **What different kinds of materials are there in the Old Testament?**

The thirty-nine (39) books listed below are those we hold in the Old Testament to be its portion of all those which contain all things necessary to salvation.[9] The material types and the books follow.

a. **The Pentateuch—Five Books of the Law.** Pentateuch is the Greek for five books. Genesis, Exodus, Leviticus, Numbers, Deuteronomy.
b. **The Twelve Historical Books**. Joshua, Judges; Ruth; I and II Samuel, I and II Kings; I and II Chronicles; Ezra; Nehemiah; Esther.
c. **Five Poetical Books**. Job, the Psalms, Proverbs, Ecclesiastes, Song of Solomon.
d. **Seventeen Prophetical Books**. Isaiah, Jeremiah, Lamentations, Ezekiel, Daniel, Hosea, Joel, Amos, Obadiah, Jonah, Micah, Nahum, Habakkuk, Zephaniah, Haggai, Zechariah, Malachi.

10. **What different kinds of materials are there in the New Testament?**

a. **Gospels**. Matthew, Mark, and Luke are called Synoptic Gospels, meaning they are alike. John, the Fourth Gospel is different.
b. **Historical**. Acts of the Apostles
c. **Epistles**
   (1) Epistles of Paul. The Epistles of Paul will be listed with dates written: I and II

Thessalonians (A.D. 51), Galatians (A.D. 48-49), I Cor. (A.D. 55), II Cor. (A.D. 56), Rom. (A.D. 57), Philemon, Colossians, Ephesians, Philippians (A.D. 61-62), I Timothy, Titus, II Timothy (A.D. 64).

(2) **Epistle to the Hebrews**.

(3) **General Epistles**. I and II Peter (A.D. 63-64) James (A.D. 60), I, II, III John (A.D. 90-100) Jude (A.D. 70-80)

d. **Apocalyptic** (A-pok-a-lip-tic). Revelation which means unveiling. It intends to unveil the Last Things. It was written about A.D. 96.[10]

SIN

1. **What is sin?**

Let us look first at **how** the Bible says sin came into the world. Paul wrote that "by one man sin entered into the world" (Rom. 5:12). The one man was Adam (Rom. 5:14).

The sin of Adam which was **an act** of disobedience provides us with an important clue in our search for a definition of sin. One, there was a standard for measuring obedience. A mark to be hit or a line to be toed. Which simply put was to not do what God had said "Don't you do." On the positive side the standard included what God said, "This you may do." There was a large area of permissive fruit that Adam and Eve could eat. And there was one fruit which was on the tree of the knowledge of good and evil that was not to be eaten (Gen. 3).

Two, at the time at least when Genesis was written desire was not sin provided it was not acted upon. Jesus, however, changed that, if desire was in fact a missing ingredient (see Matt. 5:21-48 and James 1:14-15). So, sin in Genesis included an **act**. One that specifically violated the law of God.

Three, sin breaks more than the law of God. It strains or breaks essential relationships (see Psalm 51). In Genesis the God-human being bond was broken, which is symbolized by Adam and Eve hiding when they heard what here-to-fore had been welcome footsteps walking in the Garden. Also, the harmony between Adam and Eve was beset by disharmony which symbolism may be seen in Adam passing the buck of responsibility for their actions to Eve and she to the serpent. It was a hot potato which neither was willing to hold. The nature of the changed situation in the Garden of Eden may be found in the man and woman discovering and being shame of their naked-ness.

The clothing which followed, the fig leaves from which they sewed together aprons for themselves symbolize the barriers existing between the human beings and God and themselves and creation. Prior to the disclosure of their naked-ness they were transparent or open in all relationships and sin rendered opaque that which had been clear and open.

Four, the sin of disobedience by Adam and Eve left a legacy of consequences. Sin has its effects upon the fabric of existence and life. Paul wrote that the sin of Adam brought death into the world and willed death to all because all have sinned (Rom. 5:12).

2. **You talked of sin as act, is that all there is to sin?**

I hasten to add that I really prefer to put *sin as a condition* before *sin as an act*. And I prefer *sins* when speaking of act and *sin* when speaking of the state or the condition of humanity. From sin as the human state of being turned inward worshipping and serving the creature and not the Creator (Rom. 1:25), sins are committed by thought, word and deed.

3. **What is original sin?**

The Article of Religion On Original or Birth-Sin states that it "standeth not in the falling of Adam (as the Pelagians do vainly talk)." Where, then, does it stand?

"It is the corruption of the nature of every man, that naturally is engendered of the offspring of Adam."[11] Thus, what Adam did is not the source of original sin. Rather, the consequence of his act was the corruption of human nature which is passed along by conception (See Ps. 51:5).

For many Christians if original sin means original guilt upon generations which followed Adam's sin, they argue that to be held responsible by association as human beings for Adam's sin is unfair. They see an inexcusable inequity if the only sin is they were born human. So, without violating Scripture they maintain that original sin means that every human being sins for himself and for herself. Sharing with Adam the God given freedom to choose each of us chooses to act contrary to God's will. Rather than permitting God center stage each of us seeks it for ourselves. Human beings, then, seem to lean toward sin or to have a propensity for sin. Which if true, would raise the question of "Why." Except we may be well-served to consider the oft discussed issue whether the Fall was *up* or *down*. Did it open the door to human creativity and individual growth? Or was it the loss of a perfect and complete state of being and existence that Christianity promises in the world to come?

4. **May a person sin after being "saved"?**

We believe that one may fall into sin after justification. "After we have received the Holy Ghost, we may depart from grace given, and fall into sin."[12]

The problems of understanding arise for some of us when we read in the Bible that "whosoever is born of God sinneth not" (I John 5:18). And the matter may be made more troublesome with the words, "If we say that we have no sin, we deceive ourselves, and the truth is not in us" (I John 1:8). How may we approach the dilemma?

John Wesley stated in his memorial sermon to George Whitfield in 1770 that "the two men had never differed on the central doctrine of the evangelical awakening. that the gift of the Holy Spirit in the experience of regeneration delivered believers from both the dominion and the guilt of sin and enabled them 'to walk as Christ also walked'."[13]

I venture to say that Wesley's words "delivered believers from both the dominion and guilt of sin" provide the clue to the paradox. Sin is sin only where it leads to death. For the regenerated sin cannot work its ultimate work, the work of death. "If any man sin, we have an advocate with the Father, Jesus Christ the righteous" (I John 2:1). The sins of the redeemed have been covered by Christ and they are "in him" who keeps them from the ultimate power of sin. "He is the propitiation for our sins, and not for ours only, but also for the sins of the whole world" (I John 2:2).

5. **Are you saying that by "confessing our sins" and being forgiven we have not "really sinned"?**

The weight of the New Testament falls on the side of the position which asserts that "we have the heavenly treasure in earthen vessels" (II Cor. 4:7).

This position suggests that human beings sin though they are "in Christ" (II Cor. 5:17). The difference is that Christ is our protection from sin and our advocate after we have sinned. Christ who knew no sin God "made him to be sin" and the purpose is: "so that in him we might become the righteousness of God" (II Cor. 5:21).

So, what I mean is that God in Christ has provided forgiveness for the sins of all who are made new "in Christ." By Christ taking upon himself the sin of sinful humanity he freed us from sin. We who arc "in Christ" may and do sin but when a sinner who has been saved by grace sins its effect is not terminal. That is, provided the individual exercises the option to seek forgiveness. If, however, forgiveness is not sought, the person does indeed fall from grace.

6. **Will you restate what is meant by the saying, "Whosoever is born of God does not commit sin" (I John 3:9)?**

This verse of Scripture gets to the heart of our discussion. John Wesley wrote that being "born of God" is an inward change within the soul that is wrought by the Holy Ghost. It brings about living "in quite another manner than we did before; we are, as it were, in another world."[14]

The "born of God" is sensible of God; the individual is conscious of God's real presence and the relationship between God and the human being is of such the individual "hears and knows the heavenly calling". God is known to be the source of life and more especially is He known as the One who continually gives the gracious influence of his Spirit which the human being also gives back to Him "in unceasing love, and praise, and prayer; not only doth not commit sin, while he thus keepeth himself, but so long as this "seed remaineth in him, he cannot sin because he is born of God."[15]

What does Wesley understand by "sin" in this context? He wrote, saying, "By sin I understand outward sin, according to the plain, common acceptance of the word; an actual, voluntary transgression of the law, of the revealed, written law of God".[16] But as long as a person believes in God through Christ, and loves him, and is pouring out his heart before him, Wesley wrote of such a person "he cannot voluntarily transgress any command of God."

So you ask: "Does this assertion by Mr. Wesley square with the history of experience as recorded in the Bible?" No, it does not. And Wesley was very well aware that difficulty would occur in its acceptance. He wrote that those whom we cannot deny had been truly born of God "did transgress the plain, known laws of God, speaking or acting what they knew he had forbidden?"[17] He cited such evidence as David's sin (See II Samuel 11:2ff), and of Paul's confrontation with Peter over the latter's double life (Acts 10:28, Gal. 2:11ff).

How then is it to be explained if it does not square with the experiences of all those who were saved? Wesley held rigidly to the words "he that is begotten of God keepeth himself, and that wicked one toucheth him not" (I John 5:18). This a believer is unable to do alone but can do by the grace of God. And "If he keepeth not himself, if he abideth not in the faith, he may commit sin even as another man."[18]

As you can see by not keeping him the believer may commit sin. In a sense the individual who sins is not "in Christ" because of having fallen "into *negative*, inward sin, not 'stirring up the gift of God which was in him', not 'pressing on to the mark of the prize of the high calling':'' And from inward sin, the person moved ''into *positive* inward sin, inclining to wickedness with his heart, giving way to some evil desire or temper: Next, he lost his faith, his sight of a pardoning God, and consequently his love of God, and being then weak and like another man, he was capable of commiting even *outward* sin''.[19]

7. **Does sin precede or follow the loss of faith?**

This is a question that John Wesley raised and answered.[20] His answer was: ''Some sin of omission, at least, must necessarily precede the loss of faith; some inward sin: But the loss of faith must precede the committing outward sin.''

Wesley must be understood as one who believed that once a person has been saved there must be a nurturing of the presence of God within one's being. In this way we can see why he included in the General Rules ''It is expected of all who desire to continue in these societies that they should continue to evidence their desire of salvation. Thirdly, by attending upon all the ordinances of God.''[21]

The desire for salvation was a continuing expectation of all who desired to remain with the United Societies. Their initial salvation, justification and the new birth, and baptism, is insufficient because salvation like life is not static, but dynamic. Since salvation is of God ''it plainly appears, God does not continue to act upon the soul, unless the soul reacts upon God.''[22]

So, in the dynamics of the inter-actions between God's grace and human faith is the possibility if not the probability of a believer not sinning. Where sin is done in an outward manner Wesley held that it was preceded by the failure of a Christian to re-act to God. That Christian failed to attend upon the ordinances of God, which included, "The public worship of God, The ministry of the word, either read or expounded, The Supper of the Lord, Family and private prayer; Searching the Scriptures; and Fasting or abstinence."[23]

8. **Now, do you maintain, that the earlier position on the righteous sinning and Wesley's position are not in conflict?**

The two positions are not in conflict. The earlier just as Wesley believed and preached took seriously the human element, that is, both realized that the saved have their being in bodies of flesh and blood. Both took into consideration the possibility of the sinless life. I must add except that possibility exist universally for all Christians Jesus' sinless life would have failed to provide us with an example of achievement. In other words, it is significant that he had the occasion and the opportunity to sin. The Bible says that Christ "was in all points tempted like as we are, yet without sin" (Heb. 4:15b). His abstinence was an accomplishment and it was not due to some divine quality. Because Christ did not take on the nature of angels but of the seed of Abraham (Heb. 2:16) "he is able to help those who are exposed to temptation" (Heb. 2:18, J.B. Phillips Trans.). Having been tempted Jesus the Christ is able "to be touched by the feelings of our feeble flesh" (Heb. 2:15, The N.T. in Basic English).

Where the two positions may seem to divide is where Wesley allowed that outward sin follows inward sin or the loss of faith. So in a significant way, it was not the redeemed of the Lord who sinned. Rather the sinner is one who is no longer in faith.

The earlier position held that the redeemed of the Lord may sin and for the reason that Wesley held to inward sin, and remember that is still sin, though it precedes outward sin, I do not see any conflict. Beyond sinning as an act the first position is that sin has no death power or no ultimate power provided forgiveness and reconciliation are sought.

Let me add that it is risky in building doctrine to disregard the weight of human experience as well as other statements in the Bible. A statement that has meaning to this discussion is Romans 4:8. Several translators have dealt with the verse of Scripture. Goodspeed put it in these words. "Happy is the man whose sin the Lord will take no account of." Charles B. Williams in "The New Testament: A Translation in the Language of the People" translated the verse, thus, "Happy are they whose sin the Lord does not charge against him."

In this context Paul dealt with sin as having been overcome by God through Jesus Christ and for the saved sin "must no longer control you" (Rom. 6:14 Goodspeed) for you are under grace. However caught in the crossfire of good and evil within us it is Christ who comes to the rescue. And "The conclusion of the matter is this: there is no condemnation for those who are united with ..." Christ (Rom. 8:1, NEB).

9. **What is the un-pardonable sin?**

Jesus said, "I tell you, every sin and blasphemy will be forgiven men, but the blasphemy against the Spirit will not be forgiven. And whoever says a word against the Son of man will be forgiven; but whoever speaks against the Holy Spirit will not be forgiven, wither in this age or the age to come'' (Matt. 12:31-32).

Speaking against the Holy Spirit is to despise the workings of God that He has laid on one's conscience. It is willful disobedience, whereas, a word against the Son of man may be spoken out of ignorance or misunderstanding. It is un-pardonable because of the hardened heart that fights against faith. Jesus did not deal directly with what can happen when there is a change in the condition of the heart. So, in the final analysis, the sin is unforgiven because the hard of heart will not change (Acts 7:51).

It would be unfortunate for us to conclude that the possibility of ''an un-pardonable sin'' renders grace less than effective. As I understand the matter it is not a question of whether ''where sin abounded, grace did much more abound'' (Rom. 5:20 KJB). Rather the question is on whether or not the Holy Ghost will be allowed to do His work of testifying of Jesus (John 15:26);of sin because the people do not believe in Jesus (John 16:9), of his glorification (John 16:14); and of making known that he is Lord (Rom. 8:9), without which one cannot be saved, thus, cannot be forgiven. So to blaspheme against the Spirit or to speak profanely against him is to deny the Holy Ghost his necessary place and function in salvation, which work includes regeneration and sanctification.

''Even the Spirit of true knowledge'' (John 14:17),[24] according to Jesus, ''the world cannot receive'' and there are reasons. The world ''neither sees nor knows him'' (John 14:17b, RSV). So the world ''neither observes nor understands'' the Spirit who is critical to its life. But the disciples are not of the world so they know him and ''he is with you now and will be in your hearts'' (John 14:17c, Phillips). Hearts hardened cannot contain him who makes us alive through the blood that Jesus shed. Neither can such hearts be forgiven for they attribute the work of the Lord, Jesus the Christ, to the power of the Devil (Matt. 12:24-28) and not by the Spirit of God. If Jesus did not do his works by the Spirit of God but by "Beelzebub the prince of the devils" then Satan would be divided against himself. But because he casts out demons by the Spirit of God "this is a sign that in some sense the Reign of God has already broken in upon the world."[25]

In fact Jesus told his disciples that by virtue of the Spirit of God working through him to cast out devils "then the kingdom of God is come unto you" (Matt. 12:28b). So evil speaking against the Holy Ghost is related critically to the ability of individuals to repent and receive the forgiveness that is necessary for them to return to God. Jesus is the means by whom and through whom God worked to overcome sin and evil, of him there may be ignorance and misunderstanding. So "whosoever speaketh a word against the Son of Man, it shall be forgiven him" (Matt. 12:32a). But "whoever speaks against the Holy Spirit will not be forgiven, either in this age or in the age to come" (Matt. 12:32b). This willful blindness and stubborness of heart which calls light the darkness and refuses in its "obdurate pride" to acknowledge the witness of the Spirit of God is tantamount to committing "moral suicide."

SALVATION

1. **What does "salvation" mean?**

Salvation in the noun forms as used in the New Testament means (a) material and temporal deliverance from danger and apprehension. For (1) national deliverance (Luke 1:69, 71, Acts 7:25); (2) personal deliverance as from the sea (Acts 27:34) or from prison (Phil. 1:19); (b) the spiritual and eternal deliverance granted immediately by God to those who accept His conditions of repentance and faith in the Lord Jesus, in whom alone it is to be obtained (Acts 4:12), and upon confession of Him as Lord (Rom. 10:10) for this purpose the gospel is the saving instrument (Rom. 1:16; Eph. 1:13).[26] These meanings do, I trust, provide answers that shed light upon the question. But let me add a third meaning which uses salvation as inclusive of all of God's blessings bestowed upon us in Christ by the Holy Ghost (See, II Cor. 6:2; Heb. 5:9; I Peter 1:9, 10).[27]

2. **In what restricted sense do Christians use the word "salvation"?**

The so called limited or restricted sense refers to salvation as deliverance from sin and death. Paul pointed to the relationship of sin and death in his references to death as the wages of sin (Rom. 6:23) and when he confessed to the inward struggle taking place in his soul he raised the question "who shall deliver me from the body of this death?" (Rom. 7:25).

It cannot be denied that the limited view of salvation as reference to human beings is widely intended when using the word but Paul used language that must not escape us. He wrote that "the whole creation waits with eager longing for the revealing of the sons of God, for the creation was subjected to futility" and "the whole creation itself will be set free from its bondage to decay and obtain the glorious liberty of the children of God." Along with "the whole creation that has been groaning in travail together until now'' Paul said ''we ourselves'' who ''groan inwardly as we wait for adoption as sons, the redemption of our bodies. For in this hope we are saved'' (Rom. 8:18-25).

Salvation embraces all of existence and life which God denounced (Gen. 3:17-19) and which curse He overcomes by creating ''a new heaven and a new earth'' (Isa. 65:17; Rev. 21:1).

For fear that the limited or restricted use of salvation may get short changed, I hasten to point out that death, which is the wages of sin, is more than the termination of a life. For that reason, Paul called death ''the last enemy to be destroyed'' (I Cor. 15:26). The impact of death as God's enemy may be seen in the fear it creates and thereby it subjects human beings to a lifetime of bondage (Heb. 2:15). The bondage to the fear of death causes us as human creatures to be anxious about life's meaning and purpose and it causes us to wonder whether death has the last word to render void the life that we have lived on the faith that we are part of a larger plan (II Cor. 6:1) and because of God we hope that in Christ His plan will ultimately be complete. Our joy and our peace are due to our having hope in Christ both in this life and in the life to come (I Cor. 15.19).

3. **Is a Savior necessary for salvation to become reality?**

This question is answered on the assumption that it means a savior who is other than the one being saved. In the Apostles' Creed we affirm our faith in such a Savior each time we say, ''I believe, ... in Jesus Christ, the *only* Savior, our Lord ...''

From the time the angel Gabriel was sent from God to Nazareth in Galilee to tell Mary that she would conceive and give birth to a son who she shall name Jesus (Luke 1:31) there was hope that he would indeed be the great one and the one who "shall be called the Son of the Highest", the one to whom "the Lord God shall give the throne of David" (Luke 1:32).

Jesus of Nazareth was in the Gospel according to Matthew the one who "shall save his people from their sins" (Matt. 1:21). And from the lips of those who came to Jacob's well at Sychar we hear the words of testimony which they spoke to the woman who first brought them word of the all knowing man she had met, saying, "Now we believe not because you told us of him but we believe because we heard him speak ourselves and we know now that this is without a doubt the Christ, the Savior of the world" (John 4:42, My paraphrasing.).

John the Evangelist wrote of what the apostles preached regarding Jesus. Based upon their experience he wrote, saying, "And we have seen and do testify that the Father sent the Son to be the Saviour of the world" (I John 4:14). In response to an inquiry before the Sandhedrin Council, Peter and the other apostles told its members that God exalted Jesus whom He raised from the dead "to be a Prince and a Saviour, for to give repentance to Israel and forgiveness of sins" (Acts 5:31).

Paul wrote of Jesus' humility, of his abasing of pride and of his obedience by dying on a cross, saying that God responded by exalting Jesus and bestowed upon him a peculiar or unique name (Phil. 2:9). And Peter made a bold and peculiar or unique claim for Jesus Christ of Nazareth. He told the high priest, Annas, and his colleagues that "there is salvation in no one else, for there is no other name under heaven given among men by which we must be saved" (Acts 4:12).

4. **How is a person saved?**

Let me answer this question by saying up front that Jesus has saved the world. His words from the cross on Calvary, "It is finished" (John 19:30), attest to his having done all things necessary for salvation. So when we talk of being saved or as some individuals say "getting saved" we are really talking about entering into a reality that exists already. It is similar to saying "I'm going inside to get warm." The meaning of going inside to get warm is based upon the conviction that the heat for warming does exist inside. Being saved is based upon the assumption that salvation is available and that salvation exists because of a Saviour.

Paul said that getting inside of the existing realm of salvation (Eph. 2:1-7) is done by the interaction of grace and faith. He wrote that, " *by* grace you have been saved *through* faith" (Eph. 2:8, Emphasis mine). Phillips in his translation of Eph. 2:8 made it very clear that being saved "was nothing you could or did achieve—it was God's gift of grace which saved you." Even human "faith comes from what is heard and what is heard comes by the preaching of Christ" (Rom. 10:17).

Are you saying that human beings are saved without doing anything? Of course not. What I am saying is that when God sent Jesus to save us in our sin and from our sins we were indeed helpless to help ourselves. "At the very time when we were still powerless, then Christ died for the wicked"(Rom. 5:8, *New English Bible*). By his power of love which comes to us by the preaching of Christ crucified (I Cor. 1:20-25) the Holy Ghost enables and empowers us to confess with our lips that Jesus is Lord and to believe in our hearts that God raised him from the dead thus, we are saved (Rom. 10.5-13).

5. **Can we know that we are saved? If so, how?**

John Wesley preached of "an assurance of our present pardon; not, ..., of our final perseverance."[28] Wesley recorded in his *Journals* an experience he had with a zealous opposer of "this way" on Saturday, September 30, 1738. The man had participated in the means of grace yet he had not been able to overcome his drunkenness. Mr. Wesley asked that they pray together. After a short while the man arose, his sad countenance had given way to signs of joy and peace. And he said, "Now I know God loveth *me*, and has forgiven *my* sins. And sin shall not have dominion over me; for Christ hath set me free." John Wesley commented, thusly, on the man's revelation, "And according to his faith it was unto him."[29]

Assurance of pardon, thus, of forgiveness, is a matter of trust in the faithfulness of God to do according to His Word.

Wesley taught that the sense of justification, or, the sense of having been put right before God is not always immediately known to an individual. To put it in Wesley's words, I quote him, to wit, "He may not have, till long after, the full assurance of faith, which excludes all doubt and fear."[30]

On the other hand, in a letter written to a Mr. John Smith, dated September 28, 1795, Mr. Wesley said, "I do not deny that God imperceptibly works in some a gradually increasing assurance of his love, but I am equally certain, he works in others a full assurance thereof in one moment. And I suppose, however, this godly assurance be wrought, it is easily discernible from bare reason or fancy."[31]

As we move beyond the question of whether assurance of forgiveness, pardon, and justification is instantly or gradually given, it is clear that we can and do know provided we are in Christ (II Cor. 5:17). The way we know is, "all who are led by the Spirit of God are sons of God" (Rom. 8:14), and, "When we cry, Abba! Father! it is the Spirit himself bearing witness with our spirit that we are children of God, ..." (Rom. 8:15b-16). Assurance is from God and it results from the linking together of His Spirit with our spirit by grace through faith.

6. **What are the discerning marks of the saved?**

The Article of Religion on "Of Good Works" states that: "Although good works, which are the fruits of faith, and follow after justification, cannot put away our sins, and endure the severity of God's judgment; yet are they pleasing and acceptable to God in Christ, and spring out of a true and lively faith, insomuch that by them a lively faith may be as evidently known, as a tree discerned by its fruit."[32]

I wish to expand on the meaning of fruit by turning to John Wesley's writings. He described "real Christians" in a very short verse of Scripture.[33] Paul wrote to the Church at Corinth the words Wesley used. Namely, "We walk by faith, not by sight" (II Cor. 5:7). In order to walk by faith one "must *live* by faith." Sight living is *sense* living. Living by faith means regulating all judgments concerning good and evil with reference "to things visible and eternal."

"Religion," for Wesley was "no less than living in eternity, and walking in eternity; and hereby walking in the love of God and man, in lowliness, meekness, and resignation."[34] For one who placed emphasis upon harmlessness and morality and formality or the exact observance of all the ordinances of God, Wesley placed all of these below this question. "in the name of God, by what standard do you judge of the value of things? by the visible or the invisible world?.''[35]

Those who walk by faith are not accepted by God for their works. But Wesley maintained that Methodists held the view that ''we are not saved without works, that works are a condition (though not the meritorious cause) of final salvation. It is by faith in the righteousness and blood of Christ that we are enabled to do all good works; and it is for the sake of these that all who fear God and work righteousness are accepted of him.''[36]

As I have noted the value judgment upon what we do is based on the standard of: To what do we look. Do we look on the visible or the invisible? the temporal or the eternal? And the answer given is determined by our being in faith or our not living by faith. Yet, the works never cause salvation as acts of readiness before justification. Works are a condition of final salvation.'' Again, notice the dynamic nature of salvation. In order for grace to be ultimately effective in a sanctifying way the regenerated ''must work out your own salvation in fear and trembling; for it is God who works in you, inspiring both the will and the deed, for his own chosen purpose'' (Phil. 2:12-13, N.E.B.)

7. **What is meant by ''justification''?**

Justify ''denotes the act of pronouncing righteous.'' To be justified a person has been established ''as just by acquittal from guilt.'' In Romans 4:25, Paul wrote that Jesus our Lord ''was put to death for our trespasses and raised for our justification.'' His death on Calvary did all that God required as the propitiation or as the act of re-establishing all of creation in His favor, and ''His resurrection was the confirmatory counterpart.''[37]

Justification is "the free gift in the grace of that one man Jesus Christ" which follows many trespasses due to one man's, Adam's trespass (Rom. 5:15-17). So that "as one man's trespass led to condemnation for all men, so one man's act of righteousness leads to acquittal and life for all men" (Rom. 5:18).

Faith is the means by which "we are justified" (Rom. 5:1). But do not get the impression that faith is a human invention. Paul stated the supporting truth, thus, "they are justified by his grace as a gift, through the redemption which is in Christ Jesus, whom God put forward as an expiation by his blood, to be received by faith" (Rom. 5:24-25).

God the Righteous One is the Justifier (Rom. 8:33) of "him who has faith in Jesus" (Rom. 5:26). And a person "is justified by faith apart from the works of law" (Rom. 5:28). Sin is ultimately against God (Ps. 51:1) and He alone can acquit. God is the One who also provided for our acquittal in that He did not spare His own Son "but gave him up for us all" (Rom. 8:32).

During the earthly life and ministry of Jesus he "told this parable to some who trusted in themselves." It was the parable of two men who went up to the temple to pray, one a Pharisee and the other a tax collector. The Pharisee prayed exalting his virtuous and pious life. The tax collector, on the other hand, "standing afar off, would not lift his eyes to heaven, but beat his breast, saying, 'God be merciful to me, a sinner!'." In his commentary on the outcome of the two men Jesus said that the tax collector and not the Pharisee "went down to his house justified." And he spoke words that told of the human spirit that beget God's forgiving and restoring love. He said, "every one who exalts himself will be humbled, but, he who humbles himself will be exalted'' (Luke 18:9-14). His own life proved true his words (Phil. 2:1-11).

8. **Is justification and regeneration and the new birth all one and the same?**

It is possible to use justification as a noun meaning the consequence of what God has wrought in Jesus Christ and have it mean the same as regeneration in the sense that it too as a noun describes the state of being that exists for those who are in Christ by faith.

Wesley's position on justification and the new birth was that the two ''are, in point of time, inseparable from each other, yet are they easily distinguished, as being not the same, but things of a widely different nature. Justification implies only a relative, the new birth a real, change. God in justifying us does something *for* us; in begetting us again, he does the work *in* us.'' The distinction he carries further by relating justification to that which changes our outward relation to God from enemies to children, and by the new birth ''our innermost souls are changed, so that of sinners we become saints.'' In the different natures justification restores the believer to the favor of God and the new birth restores the believer to the image of God. Justification takes away guilt, the new birth takes away the power of sin.[38]

New birth is used of spiritual regeneration. It communicates a new life which Paul stated, thus, ''he saved us, not because of deeds done by us in righteousness, but in virtue of his own mercy, by the washing of regeneration, and the renewal of the Holy Spirit'' (Titus 3:5).

W. E. Vine wrote that "The new birth and regeneration do not represent successive stages in spiritual experience, they refer to the same event but view it in different aspects." The new birth stresses the new spiritual life that is communicated to the believer, thus, doing away with the old life (II Cor. 5:17, Gal. 2:20). Regeneration lays stress upon the inception of a new state of things in contrast with the old. Jesus used the words "in the new world, when the Son of man shall sit on his glorious throne, ..." (Matt. 19:28) in the wider sense of the "restoration of all things" (Acts 3:21 K.J.B.). Which use sets forth the meaning of regeneration as the beginning of the new state of the Reign of God.[39]

From what I have written it is obvious that while justification, new birth and regeneration may be used as references to the same event, they are not identical in meaning. They may start at the same point but they diverge with each stressing a specific aspect of meaning.

9. **What is the meaning of "conversion?"**

In Acts 15:3 Luke wrote that Paul and Barnabas "passed through both Phoenicia and Samaria, reporting the conversion of the Gentiles." Which points to the meaning of turning about, or turning round. In a more complete sense conversion implies "a turning *from* and a turning *to*. Corresponding to these are repentance and faith."[40] Paul wrote to the Church of the Thessalonians and said that word of their faith had gone everywhere that is, "how you turned to God from serving idols, to serve a true and living God" (I Thess. 1:9).

Erik Routley wrote that "In the Bible, "convert" means "turn." And in this word "turn" there is always a dramatic force. It is a decisive turning that follows stopping in your tracks, then turning and going in a new direction. "When Peter in his sermon to the Jews recorded in Acts 3 said (v. 19), 'Repent therefore and turn again,' he meant something quite decisive"[41] Peter meant "Stop. You are going the wrong way. Listen to my words. Turn and go the way I have told you of."

10. **What is the role of repentance in the turning?**

Repentance "signifies to change one's mind or purpose, always in the New Testament, involving a change for the better, an amendment, and always, except in Luke 17:3, 4, of repentance from sin."[42]

Repentance may seem like a purely human act but it is not without God setting the requirement for turning from sin. John the Baptist said to the Pharisees and Sadducees coming to him for baptism, "You brood of ripers! Who warned you to flee from the wrath to come? Bear fruit that befits repentance?" (Matt. 3:7-8). According to John the Baptist the urgency of repentance was "the kingdom of heaven is at hand" (Matt. 3:2). Readiness for entry into it required a change of mind and that was not easy for the Pharisees and Sadducees who said, "We have Abraham as our Father" (Matt. 3:9). Neither is repentance easy for anyone who claims protection by virtue of position, possessions, or heritage or any other refuge.

So John demanded that those who came to him for baptism show by their lives signs of changed minds. For the Jews that may have meant not appealing to the fatherhood of Abraham but of throwing themselves upon the mercy of God.

I started out addressing the concern of whether repentance is a totally human act. If Paul's words may be used again, I will say that God gives repentance or He leads us to it. Truthfully, it is difficult to pinpoint in matters spiritual where God's part ends and where human effort begins. So even after I put the question before you which Paul asked Christians at Rome, namely, "Do you not know that God's kindness is meant to lead you to repentance?" (Rom. 2:4b), it appears that human beings looking upon God's goodness must have the good conscience and the spirit of contrition that leads them to repent rather than to continue on with the same old mind set, which nature is captured by Paul's kindred question to the one above: "do you presume upon the riches of his kindness and forbearance and patience?" (Rom 2:4a).

I do not wish to put forth unbiblical information on the relationship of repentance and conversion. But let me say that repentance is the change of mind that conversion demonstrates by one's turning from Satan to God. Repentance, if I may, is inward and conversion is outward. In a real sense both are part of regeneration and the new birth. Repentance is the result of a heart convicted of the need to change and conversion is the act of turning round which translates a subjective or inward decision into an objective and outward display thereby demonstrating "fruit worthy of repentance."

11. **What is meant by "sanctification"?**

Let us regard salvation as a journey in pursuit of a destination. The destination is maturity in the likeness of Christ (Eph. 4:15). It is growth in the grace and knowledge of the Lord (II Pet. 3:18). And with the thought of a journey in mind, "The whole process of keeping, or being kept to the road, is sanctification."[43]

John Wesley, in his first conference which began Monday, June 25, 1744 with six clergymen and all of his preachers present, answered the question "What is it to be sanctified?" with these words, "To be renewed in the image of God, in righteousness and true holiness."[44] On August 1, 1745 in his second conference he said that sanctification begins "In the moment a man is justified. (Yet sin remains in him, yea, the seed of all sin, till he is sanctified throughout). From that time a believer gradually dies to sin, and grows in grace."[45]

For Wesley sanctification could be partial and for that reason and more important for the reason that Jesus said, "You, therefore, must be perfect, as your heavenly Father is perfect" (Matt. 5:48) he advocated that his preachers "speak almost continually of the state of justification; but more rarely, 'at least in full and explicit terms, concerning entire sanctification'." A reality promised of God (I John 3:8, Eph. 5:25-27, Rom. 8:3-4).[46]

Methodist preachers were expected to preach total sanctification to those who were pressing on but in a way whereby they might be drawn and not driven to "Entire sanctification, or Christian perfection" which "is neither more nor less than pure love, love expelling sin, and governing both the heart and life of a child of God. The refiner's fire purges out all that is contrary to love, and that many times by a pleasing smart."[47]

12. **Assuming that all of this is the making one Christian, if so, what is a Christian?**

"What makes Christians different is Christ. A Christian is one who belongs to Christ, one whose ways of feeling, thinking, and acting are determined by Christ."[48] The pull of this definition is toward Paul and his classical saying, "If anyone is in Christ, he is a new creation, ..." (II Cor. 5:17) and it is toward Paul again wherein he wrote to the church at Galatia giving a personal testimony, saying to them, "I have been crucified with Christ: the life I now live is not my life but the life which Christ lives in me; and my present bodily life is lived by faith in the Son of God who loved me and sacrificed himself for me" (Gal. 2:20).

Being Christian is not being merely religious or pious or saved privately in isolation from the fellowship of the community of the redeemed of God. Being Christian means being part of the body of Christ and being individually members of the body the Christian is at the same time unavoidably members one with every other member. As Paul put it, "let every one speak the truth with his neighbor, for we are members one of another" (Eph. 4:25). Also Paul wrote to the Corinthians these words, "We, though many, are one body in Christ, and individually members one of another" (Rom. 12:5).

Finally, Wesley is reported to have said, "Christianity is essentially a social religion: and to turn it into a solitary one is to destroy it."[49]

13. **So, the Christian is a person in the faith by the grace of God who is in the process of going on to perfection?**

I have so contended, even if subtly so. From Scripture and experience it is obvious to me that the most saintly and respected and admired Christian men and women, have weaknesses and sins that cling closely. This truth, however, does not make them non-Christian. But it is truth that motivates them to "press on toward the goal for the prize of the upward call of God in Christ Jesus" (Phil. 3:14).

I close with two quotes from John Wesley.[50]

> "I would have you, not almost, but altogether, a Christian. You cannot be content with less. You cannot be satisfied with right notions; neither with harmlessness; no, nor yet with barely external religion, how exact soever it be. Neither will you be content with just a taste of inward religion."

> "A taste of love cannot suffice, Your soul for all his fullness cried." Exhort the believers everywhere to "go on to perfection"; otherwise, they cannot keep what they have."

14. **If being saved is the starting point for this process: "What must I do to be saved?"**

To me the Scriptures are clear on the answer to this question. Unfortunately, so much baggage, so many requirements have been tacked on to what is a gift to be received. What could be more plain than the words, "Believe in the Lord Jesus, and you will be saved, you and your household" (Acts 16:31).

In our hands no price we bring for "we were reconciled to God by the death of his Son" and His grace though costly is not free and "now that we are reconciled, shall we be saved by his life" (Rom. 5:10). Receive the gift. Believe the promise. Trust the Giver.

Chapter IV

BASIC BELIEFS-B

INTRODUCTION

1. **What is a sacrament?**

For Protestants generally the chief problem in understanding the sacraments is to understand the relationship between the sign and the thing signified. Some brief and helpful definitions have come down to us through the writings of the Churchmen and Reformers. The sacrament is "a physical sign of a spiritual reality." The sacrament is "the external sign of an inner reality." Sacraments have been called "the visible word." Just as we have an "audible word" which conveys the promises and benefits of Christ to a believer, so we have in the sacrament a "visible word" which conveys Christ and his benefits.[1]

I have held to a definition of a sacrament consistent with the above. It has been part of our heritage. It states that. A sacrament is an outward and visible sign of an inward and spiritual grace.

2. **How many sacraments, do we accept in the C.M.E. Church?**

We subscribe to two (2) sacraments. They are Baptism and Holy Communion or the Lord's Supper.

3. **Your answer to the question of the number of Sacraments implies that there are more than two. True?**

Yes. There are more than two practiced in the Roman Catholic Church. But let me share with you what Article 16 of the Articles of Religion says on the matter.

"There are two sacraments ordained of Christ our Lord in the Gospel; that is to say, Baptism and the Supper of our Lord.

"Those five commonly called sacraments—that is to say Confirmation, Penance, Orders, Matrimony, and Extreme Unction—are not to be counted for Sacraments of the Gospel, being such as have partly grown out of the corrupt following of the apostles and partly are states of life allowed in the Scriptures, but yet have not the like nature of Baptism and the Lord's Supper, because they have not any visible sign or ceremony ordained of God.

"The sacraments were not ordained of Christ to be gazed upon, or to be carried about; but that we should duly use them. And in such only as worthily receive the same, they have a wholesome effect or operation; but they that receive them unworthily, purchase to themselves condemnation as Saint Paul saith, I Cor. xi. 29."[2]

4. **On what basis do we limit ourselves to only two sacraments?**

In the Article of Religion quoted above the opening sentence is critical to answering this question. Let me restate it in part. "There are two sacraments *ordained of Christ our Lord* in the Gospel; ..." The emphasis placed upon selected words indicates the importance of Jesus having ordained or instituted a sacrament. His ordination is basic and fundamental to its acceptance and practice. So what the Article of Religion holds is that the other five "have not any visible sign or ceremony ordained of God."

Sacraments in the Christian Church have always been essentially linked "historically to the episode of the incarnation, to the words and works of Jesus Christ in the days of His flesh."[3]

In light of that fact the freedom for the Church to select additional rites and call them sacraments does not exist. That is, if we take seriously the fact that Christ is *the* Sacrament. And the practice of rites which claim to communicate Christ must indeed have his blessing as manifested both in his having *ordained* the same and his having *commanded* that his followers continue to practice them.

5. **What do sacraments do?**

Sacraments express a reality that they also convey. They communicate life and life sustaining nourishment from God to the faithful in community.

The statement made earlier which said "Christ is *the* Sacrament" provides the background for sacrament as communication. "With the incarnation, God takes a human body," the body being the only means of communication that we have. In that normal fashion God communicated with us in Jesus the Christ. John called him "the Word made flesh" and he said of him that he dwelt among us "full of grace and truth" (John 1:14).

I will let a quote from Ernest J. Fielder and R. Benjamin Garrison address the tie between the sacraments and communication. Here is the quote.

> God became man. God made a physical entrance into the world. And Christ lived out his life of union with the Father by loving the world and ultimately in giving himself totally for it. In the process he was branded by a self-righteous segment of people because he "ate with sinners"; he broke obsolete laws, he shocked the complacent; he became so totally "world" that Paul finally pointed out that he became totally like us in everything "except sin." And, as we

remarked earlier, his presence is continuous, even now.

Surely he is present in the impressive pageantry of sacraments celebrated with all the ponderous dignity, awe, and precise correctness of many of our ritual enactments today. But that is because he agrees to be "all things to all men" and to be like us in everything but sin. However, the Christian church has been rather stodgy in meeting the contemporary world face-to-face. But he has stayed with us nonetheless, of course, even in such celebrations. But was such ponderous pageantry his way while physically on earth? No. He could have been rich but he chose to be poor. He could have had brass bands and "legions of angels," but he chose a donkey and the riffraff of the streets for his entry into Jerusalem. He was always simple and simply accessible, so that he could be understood by anyone who cared to receive his communications.[4]

6. **Does faith have a part to play in the sacraments?**

It must be kept in mind that "All this is God's doing" (II Cor. 5:18, Phillips). And to put faith into God's doing in such a way as to make the effects of the sacraments dependent upon human faith may cause us to neglect the fact that faith in the acceptance of God's grace is itself a gift from God. That is, let us not imagine that faith is any kind of works that we perform which can make us ready and worthy for a sacrament.

"Thus instead of saying that sacraments depend on human faith, it seems better to say that sacraments *operate through* faith.''[5] However, we are not non-persons in this correspondence. God does not act upon us arbitrarily. He works faith in our hearts ''by winning us, gaining our confidence, not forcing it.'' Just think! He loved us so much that He gave His only Son, even unto death for our salvation. His gracious love and tender mercy coming to us when we were helpless create faith. It is our faith and we go willingly to meet Him in the sacraments.

''As Baron von Hugel has written. 'I kiss my child not only because I love it; I kiss it also in order to love it. A religious picture not only expresses my awakened faith, it is a help to my faith's awakening'.''[6] So it is with the sacraments.

BAPTISM

1. **In what context does baptism belong?**

Baptism belongs in the Church. It was entrusted to the fellowship of the body of Christ's disciples (Matt. 28:19). It is important to note that Jesus the resurrected Christ placed the command to baptize disciples between the *proclamation* of his having been given all power and his *promise* to be with his disciples who went forth to fulfill his commission and his command (Matt. 28:19).

The context of baptism is the fellowship of faithful believers with whom the all-powerful Christ is present. Be mindful of the fact that the promise of Jesus the Christ to be present with his fellowship of the called out ones was not a general promise. The promise was made to a peculiar group of individuals whose association was centered in and around Jesus the

Christ. The promise was made to these peculiar people in view of their involvement in the mission and ministry given to them by Jesus the Christ. ''Lo, I am with you always'' was not given in general terms by the all-powerful Christ. He promised to be with his disciples that the ministries of making disciples, baptizing and teaching them would be effective as instruments of grace. The promise ''I am with you always'' was not without context and structure. The disciples as the called-out-ones, the Church, were the recipients of the promise from the Christ to whom all power had been given and the promise of his presence was for doing ministry.

What is the importance of this for present day baptism? First, it makes clear that prior to baptism the Church as the visible body of Christ is the setting or the context of his presence and power. Among the two or three gathered together in the name of Jesus the Christ he is present (Matt. 18:20). Grace is present in the Church and grace is present by the Holy Spirit to present and baptize and receive a little child or an adult into the Church as the body of Christ.

If we concede that grace is before faith and that grace is present to faith that does not rule out the fact that an infant cannot believe in Jesus the Christ as Savior and Lord. In an earlier section the matter of faith was discussed and made clear that the faith is that of the Church. So infant baptism is not an effort to overlook nor neglect faith. Again, infant baptism and in a more dramatic fashion than so called believer's baptism highlights grace and puts grace in its proper perspective. It shows forth human dependency upon divine grace and takes seriously the Church as the community of faithful believers in Jesus the Christ.

In Capernaum Jesus healed a paralytic that had been let down on a pallet by four men through the roof of a house where Jesus was preaching. The unusual aspect of this word of forgiveness and act of healing is not that they happened, Jesus forgave the sins of others and he also healed others of their infirmities. The unique element in this episode is the fact that it was not the faith of the paralytic that undergirded the response of Jesus to his plight. Instead Mark wrote, "And when Jesus saw *their faith*" (Mark 2:5, Emphasis mine), Jesus said to the paralytic, 'My son, your sins are forgiven'."

The same principle of the faith of another was present when Jesus healed the servant of a centurion in Capernaum. The immediate beneficiary of the centurion' s faith was the servant (Matt. 8:5-13) whom Jesus healed from afar. The daughter of the ruler who was awakened from a sleep that everyone else called death was in response to the faith of her father (Matt. 9:18-26).

What do these things mean? They mean that while faith is a partner with divine grace in the healing and helping ministry of God that faith is not always the act of the individual who is healed or helped. On the occasions mentioned above the faith of others proved sufficient to receive the expression of God's compassion and caring love.

The behavior of the Philippian jailer which led to his baptism by Paul did not lead to his baptism only, his relief led to his salvation and baptism and to the salvation and baptism of the members of his household. In that era it was commonplace for such households to consist of men, women, children, and servants.

So, the Church which itself is an expression of grace and faith is the proper setting for baptism.

2. **What is baptism?**

I want to share with you several answers to the question. Baptism: What Is It?

One, "the rite of Christian baptism may legitimately be said to be an event ('baptism as birth') as well as a process" ("baptism as life").[7]

Baptism as birth for Christians follows from the finished work of Jesus on the cross (John 19:30). On that date the world was saved.

Baptism as process is the baptized person working out the benefits of baptism, which is a life-long responsibility and privilege. By faith the baptized continues to look back to the event of his or her baptism and is blessed by the grace received.

Two, baptism is a sacrament, a means of grace, in which the recipient receives the benefits of the Gospel.[8]

Three, baptism is an initiatory rite and is a sign of the inward grace that it represents.[9]

Four, "baptism is the outward sign of this inward grace, which is supposed by our Church to be given with and through that sign to all infants, and to those of riper years, if they repent and believe the gospel."[10]

Five, "Baptism is not only a sign of profession and mark of difference, whereby Christians are distinguished from others that are not baptized; but it is also a sign of regeneration, or the new birth".[11]

3. **Where do we begin our search for more understanding of this sacrament?**

Jesus was baptized by John. Is that the proper place to begin this little talk on Christian baptism? I think not. For the reason that John's baptism was interim. It was a temporary rite and would be superseded by the baptism of the Holy Ghost (Matt. 3:11, 12).

Further, the reason that Jesus submitted to baptism by John was not the same as the Judeans who were baptized in the river Jordan confessing their sins (Matt. 3:5). Jesus who was "without sin" (Heb. 4:15) was baptized by John "to fulfill all righteousness" (Matt. 3:15). Which meant at least that the Scriptures might be fulfilled and in the second instance that Jesus might identify with his people. By this act his empathy and his identification with Israel placed him at one with humanity. "Since, therefore, the children share in flesh and blood, he himself likewise partook of the same nature ... For surely it is not with angels that he is concerned but with the descendants of Abraham" (Heb. 2:14, 16).

Jesus was not baptized out of necessity due to sin but as an opportunity to "be revealed to Israel" (John 1:31).

Had John's baptism not been interim and partial Paul would not have re-baptized the twelve disciples in Ephesus who had been baptized "Into John's baptism" (Acts 19:3).

If the baptism of Jesus by John is not the place to start where do we begin? The evidence from Holy Scripture directs us to Calvary and the death of Jesus upon a cross. Prior to that Friday on 29 A.D. Jesus had received a request for personal privilege by two of his disciples, James and John. They asked to sit "one at your right hand and one at your left, in your glory." To which Jesus gave a very illuminating reply. A reply that points us to the true baptism. He said, "You do not know what you are asking. Can you drink the cup I have to drink, or undergo the baptism I have to undergo?" (Mark 10:38, Moffatt). Baptism as future experience was made known by Jesus when he said, "I have a baptism to be baptized with; and how I am constrained until it is accomplished"

The death and resurrection of Jesus are source and symbol of Christian baptism. It is source in that all are justified by the grace of God which is a gift through the redemption which is Christ Jesus (Rom. 2:24). It is symbol in "that all of us who have been baptized into Christ Jesus were baptized into his death" (Rom. 6:3). And "we were buried therefore with him by baptism into death, so that as Christ was raised from the dead by the glory of the Father, we too might walk in newness of life" (Rom. 6:4).

Paul in the Letter to the Church at Ephesus described the human condition before the death and resurrection of Jesus the Christ as "dead through the trespasses and sins" (Eph. 2:1). And by grace making alive together with Christ which is the work of God who "raised us up with him" (Eph. 2:6) point to the newness of life or that of being raised up with Christ which are symbolic of baptism, dying to sin and rising to new life.

As John Wesley taught baptism is not regeneration or the new birth. But without the death of Jesus by which the world was justified there would be no regeneration of which baptism is a sign. By virtue of the primary nature of Jesus dying on a cross and his being buried and raised from the dead therein is the starting point for Christian baptism.

4. **What modes do we use for baptism?**

In Volume 2 of *A Contemporary Wesleyan Theology*, it has been pointed out that each mode of baptism is typical of one particular aspect of the new life or "inward grace." Immersion or plunging or dipping into a fluid or into a liquid is alluded to in Romans 6:4 "Buried with him in baptism" speaks of the negative side, a death to the old life while "raised with Christ" denotes the positive side, a new life in Christ.

Sprinkling points to the provision of the sprinkled blood (Heb. 9:11-14; I Peter 1:2). Through Christ God reconciled to himself all things, "making peace by the blood of his cross" (Col. 1:20).

"The mode of pouring emphasized the life of the Holy Spirit prophesied and coming upon the believers in the Upper Room" (Joel 2:28; Acts 2:1-2, 38).[12]

If we are to avoid the trap of over emphasizing a particular mode Christian Methodists must remember, one, that in the case of each of the three modes mentioned above God's initiative precedes our faith. Two, we must keep in mind also that we may use all three modes.

However, because there are some Christians who deny the legitimacy of sprinkling and pouring some discussion of the evidence that Jesus was immersed must be entered into. And some discussion of the evidence that sprinkling is a legitimate mode of baptism must engage our time.

Was Jesus immersed in the river Jordan by John? Those who say he was immersed point to the words in Matthew's Gospel account which says "he went up immediately from the water" (3:16), or Mark's "And when he came up out of the water" (1:10).

If it could be proved that Jesus was immersed it would prove nothing. It is not the mode but the grace of God mediated through faith that is important. Because modes other than immersion are often under attack I will say some things about sprinkling.

The background for much of what will be written here is a small pamphlet that was not copyrighted and is signed "Anonymous." It gives what it calls "some reasons why a great majority of Christians in the world prefer sprinkling as their mode of water baptism."

(1) Because the inspired writers, including the prophets, Isaiah and Ezekiel, prophesied that it would be administered by sprinkling (Isa. 52:15, [KJV]; Ezek. 36:22-25).

(2) Church history shows that millions and millions of Christians have preferred sprinkling proving the truth of the prophets. (3) The one baptism referred to in the Bible is not water baptism. John did baptize with water but the important thing is the fact that Jesus baptized with the Holy Ghost and with fire (Matt. 3:11). Water baptism has never saved a soul and never will. (4) Christ was not buried in a liquid grave. "Therefore we are buried with him by baptism *into death*" (Rom. 6:4). He was buried in Joseph's new tomb. A careful reading of Romans 6:4 will show conclusively that it has reference to the death of the old man Adam in the believer, and the resurrection of the new man (the spiritual birth), carrying us right back to that one true baptism of the Holy Spirit.

(5) There is no proof except by way of mere presumption that Christ was baptized by immersion. The King James Version of the Bible states that "And Jesus, when he was baptized went up straightway out of the water ..." (Matt. 3:16a). Straightway means immediately and if it is assumed that he was put under the water and "went up straightway," what is the basis for doing so? If it means that Jesus went under the water and came up straightway did John go under the water with him? If Jesus necessarily

went under water in order for John to baptize Jesus, John necessarily went under water also.

(6) Other instances of water baptism, Paul was baptized in the *house* of Ananias, and the Scripture says he "arose" and was baptized (Acts 9:18). It is unlikely that Ananias had a baptistry in his house. The Philippian jailer and his family were baptized. This ungodly home hardly contained a baptistry (Acts 16:32-33). Cornelius and his household were baptized *in his home* (Acts 10:47, 48). Peter said on this occasion. "Can any man forbid water, that these should not be baptized, which have received the Holy Ghost as well as we?"

It is impossible to imagine the 3000 converts on the day of Pentecost who were baptized "the same day" (Acts 2:41) being baptized by immersion. If the eleven disciples would have immersed one candidate each every five minutes from about 10:00 a.m. they would have baptized 132 every hour together. By 7:00 p.m., nine hours later, they would have baptized only 1188 of the 3000. The Anonymous Author believes that Peter "most likely did it just like John the Baptizer did, with the use of that 'reed that was shaken by the wind' with hyssop or some other suitable device thereto attached, by which he sprinkled them in multiples."

He went on to write. "We have no quarrel with those good people who practice immersion, and they should have no quarrel with those who practice sprinkling" (p. 11). For the churches that practice the three modes (of which we are one) it would seem that we should be on safe ground. Not so! Some of the members of the C.M.E. Church fail to understand that baptism *with water* does not necessarily mean *in water*. And there are many thinkers and scholars who agree with Martin E. Marty who wrote that: ''There is no doubt that the early church ordinarily immersed people entirely or at least used a great deal of water.''[13] Yet it is difficult to deny that a belief in baptism as a mechanical and magical act may be the basis for a mindset that refuses to yield on the belief that baptism by immersion is the only way.

J. S. Whale quoted P. T. Forsyth in showing the emphasis in a sacrament is God and his action. ''Prayer is a gift and a sacrifice that we make: Sacrament is a gift and a sacrifice that God makes. In prayer we go to God: in Sacrament God comes to us.''[14] God is not controlled by a particular mode. And Christians should realize that ''*each* mode is a way of understanding the *whole* work of Jesus Christ as Savior. Therefore, each mode of baptism participates in the meaning of the other two, so it does not matter which mode is used.''[15]

As a reminder ''Immersion symbolizes death to self and resurrection to the new life in Christ, sprinkling symbolizes cleansing; pouring symbolizes the outpouring and overflowing of the Spirit of God.''[16]

It seems that the repentance-water-Spirit connection is more important than the mode. John Wesley wrote that ''Baptism is performed by washing, dipping, or sprinkling the person, in the name of the Father, Son, and Holy Ghost, who is hereby devoted to the ever-blessed Trinity. I say, by *washing, dipping, or sprinkling*; because it is not determined in Scripture in which of these ways it shall be done, neither by any express precept, nor by any such example as clearly provides it; nor by the force of meaning of the word baptize.''[17]

5. **Is baptism for "believers" only? What of infant baptism?**

The discussion here centers on faith and its relationship to baptism. Such discussions lead inevitably to infant baptism.

Before the infant baptism issue is dealt with let us discuss the meaning and the role of faith in baptism.

Faith is not self-created, it is a gift from God. Faith is not grace creating; it is the conduit through which grace is mediated. It is not a matter of human beings loving God but it is a matter of loving because God first loved us (I John 4:10). That order in which Divine grace comes before human faith tells us that grace is creator and giver of faith.

The Christian Church in the main has not attempted to separate grace and faith in baptism. By the same token it disavows the claim that meaning in the Sacraments is a thing apart from the finished work of Christ. What we have in the Sacrament of Baptism as in the Lord's Supper is a combining of Word and Action. It was Jesus the Christ who commanded the disciples to "Go ... make disciples ... baptizing them ..." And it was Christ who gave the promise to those who would obey "And, lo, I am with you always ..." (Matt. 28:19, 20).

The grace of God that is experienced is given through obedient response. Yet the capacity for response, the faith vessel, "comes by hearing the word of God" (Rom. 10:17). The word of God is one; "the Word became flesh," (John 1:14), in Jesus the Christ who quickens or brings to life those "who were dead in trespasses and sin" (Eph. 2:4).

Before anyone was circumcised, which was the forerunner of baptism, or before anyone received Christian baptism grace is. Not only does grace precede our having been baptized, grace had created a community of faithful believers. In fact the commission to baptize was given to the fellowship of disciples on a mountain in Galilee (Matt. 28:16). It was not given to isolated individuals but to his little church, the called out ones. And when the 3000 converts were baptized, they were added "unto them" (Acts 2:41, K.J.V.), "were added to the number of disciples" (J. B. Phillips); "were added to their number that day" (N.E.B.).

Now those who were baptized had "gladly received" the word Peter preached (Acts 2:41, K.J.V.); or "so those who received his word were baptized" (R.S.V.), or "those who welcomed his message" (Phillips), or "those who accepted his word" (N.E.B.) were baptized.

It is clear that regeneration preceded baptism. The act of baptism, a rite done to the individual, is a declaration of having accepted and received the grace of God given in Jesus the Christ. That act done by the Church as the body of Christ is Christ publicly receiving and accepting one for whom he gave his life. The baptized stands before God in Christ through the empowerment of the Holy Spirit as a new creation (II Cor. 5:17) born not of works but by grace through faith (Eph. 2:8).

What of infants who cannot believe for themselves? John Wesley wrote a very truthful statement that I share with you now. "It is certain that our Church supposes that all who are baptized in their infancy are at the same time born again; and if it is allowed that the whole Office for the Baptism of Infants precede upon this supposition. Nor is it an objection of any weight against this, that we cannot comprehend how this work can be wrought in infants.

For neither can be comprehended how it is wrought in a person of riper years.''[18]

Regeneration or having been born again or saved is a mystery. We have a description of the procedure and process, which points first to God's love for the world, a love so compelling that He gave His only Son that whoever believes in him shall not perish but have eternal life (John 3:16). Second, the Son was born, he grew to manhood, accepted the ministry of reconciliation and after three years as Son of God and Servant of humanity he died on a cross. In dying he announced regarding his work as Savior ''It is finished'' (John 19:30). All things necessary to satisfy God and to justify or to make right with Him the past and present and future of sinful humanity.

Justification is the result of the Christ-event, his incarnation, his crucifixion and resurrection which made all creation right with God. Regeneration is the new birth and while justification is universal and general regeneration is the fruit of grace and faith intersecting in the life of a human being (Eph. 2:8). The mystery in regeneration is how a once for all act, how the death of Jesus on a cross in 29 A.D. can save in the 20th Century. The mystery is not in the matter of an infant not being able to believe it is in ''the scandal of particularity,'' that is, the once and for all death of Jesus being sufficient for salvation and being effective for the same (Rom. 6:5-11; I Pet. 3:18). Another thing must be said. Admit that an adult who is able to believe for herself or for himself can be saved. Is that the real and true test of grace and faith? I say it is not. The genuine test of a Christian's ability to believe ''But with God all things are possible'' is to trust that God's grace is sufficient for the receiving of an infant into the Church through baptism.

Herein is the challenge to faith. Earlier it was stated that baptism and faith are never separated. But I do not mean that God is limited in His will to save infants because some Christians confuse individual with individu*alism*. That confused mentality suggests something short in its understanding of the Church, its nature and meaning. And with it a distorted view of baptism, grace and faith.

For many people the Church is a loose association of unrelated individuals rather than the body of Christ of which the saved in Christ are members and are also individually members one of another (Rom. 12:5; Eph. 4:25b). For some Christians faith is a human achievement and not a divinely given gift (Rom. 10:17, Gal. 3:2). Grace is the Divine response to human works and human righteousness rather than God's initiative which precedes our faith.

When faith is seen as what Fiedler and Garrison called "kindred trust" "Whose affirmation is closer to you love me than it is to 'I believe in you' or even 'I love you' then infant baptism is the appropriate mode"[19] "Believer's baptism" comes close to being works righteousness in that baptism is looked upon as a reward for faith. On the other hand, an infant presented for baptism is at the mercy of God's love.

Professor J. S. Whale who took seriously the objective givenness of the Gospel of Redemption, in the sense that Christ has redeemed all humanity, taught that the divinely given sign of this redemption is baptism. Baptism proclaims that God did something for us without consulting us and infant baptism takes seriously what God has done.

Professor Whale pointed up the three-fold significance of infant baptism. It guards against the menance of a private and inward approach to being

Christian. For again infant baptism relies upon the objective act of Christ in redemption. Second, infancy guards against the fallacy known as "dedicatory baptism." Baptism with the water of cleansing as the God-given sign, the Church proclaims the primary fact, namely, that God loves this child, and Christ died that the child might be incorporated, and not dedicated, in the great company of his redeemed. Third, infant baptism has been and is the great historical guarantee of the Church as something more than loose local associations of believers. It points up the fact that God is able to achieve in the baptism of infants that which corresponds to experience apart from personal faith. He does so through the faith of the Church and not of the child. Baptism is a real act of the church and, therefore, of Christ. The Church is his body. In the act of baptism the Church as Christ's body says what he has done and will do for the child. He baptizes the child into himself.[20]

Because we are Methodists and John Wesley is the Father of Methodism his views on infant baptism ought to be part of our background understanding. What follows is what Wesley called "the grounds of infant baptism, taken from Scripture, reason, and primitive, universal practice."

First, infants need to be washed from original sin, therefore, they are proper subjects of baptism.[21] Wesley taught that the death which Adam died due to his disobedience was a spiritual death. He was dead to God, wholly dead in sin; void of the image of God. So every child born of woman is born bearing "the image of the devil in pride and self-will." ... "Everyone that is born of a woman must be born of the Spirit of God."[22]

The Christ as the last Adam (I Cor. 15:45) has the remedy for healing the disease of corruption of the first man, Adam. Paul wrote that Christ is "the life giving spirit" (I Cor. 15:45). Reception of the remedy must be "through the means which he (God) hath appointed, through baptism in particular which is the ordinary means he hath appointed for that purpose ..."[23]

Second, if infants are capable of making a covenant, and were and still are under the evangelical covenant, then they have a right to baptism, which is the entering seal thereof. Wesley maintained that infants are both capable of making a covenant and are under the evangelical covenant.

He maintained that the Bible proved him right. Quoting Deuteronomy 29:10-12 which state: "Ye stand this day all of you before the Lord,—your captains, with all the men of Israel; your little ones, your wives and the stranger,—that thou shouldest enter into covenant with the Lord thy God." From the Hebrew Wesley held that "little ones" properly signify infants. Children, even little children, infants were and are obliged to perform at a later time what they are not capable of performing at the time of their entering into that obligation.

Wesley regarded the covenant with Abraham a gospel covenant, with obedience the inseparable fruit, its Mediator is Christ (Gen. 22:18; Gal. 3:16) and it was an everlasting covenant (Gen. 17:7; Gal. 3:7). The seal was circumcision (Acts 7:8). Baptism succeeded circumcision and the Lord's Supper took the place of the passover (Col. 2:11-13; Luke 22:15).

Third, infants are capable of coming to Christ, of admission into the Church, and solemn dedication to God.

That infants ought to come to Christ appears from the words of Jesus (Matt. 19:13, 14; Luke 18:15).

How can they come now to Christ? They can come to him only by being brought into the Church; which cannot be but by baptism.

Fourth, the Apostles baptized infants just as the Jews constantly baptized as well as circumcised all infant proselytes. The absence of any mention of infants being baptized proves nothing. The Apostles not only baptized large numbers they also baptized families, such as Gaius, Stephanas, and Crispus.

To Peter and the rest of the apostles the Jews with penitent and contrite hearts asked the question: "Brethren what shall we do?" And Peter said to them, "Repent, and be baptized every one of you in the name of Jesus Christ for the forgiveness of your sins; and you shall receive the gift of the Holy Spirit. For the promise is to you and *to your children* and to all that are far off, every one whom the Lord our God calls to him" (Acts 2:38, 39). (Emphasis mine M.G.)

Fifthly, to baptize infants has been the general practice of the Christian Church in all places and in all ages. The Apostles were close to Christ and baptized infants so the basis is sure.

6. **What does baptism do?**

There is at least one reason for asking the question: Baptism, what does it do? The reason is: There are persons who believe that baptism does something. The something done by baptism may be subjective or inner. Nonetheless, the spiritual nature of what it does makes the doing even more important to those who believe that baptism does something. By and large the doing or the work of water baptism is associated with baptism by immersion. And the act of being baptized by immersion is limited to believers, that is, to individuals who are old enough to be accountable for their own choices.

Upon close examination the issue that supports believer's baptism by the mode of immersion may be its emotional impact and not its efficacy. Many times over church members are heard to complain, saying, "I don't remember being baptized. Why can't I be baptized now that I will know what I am doing?" The majority of individuals who request to bc re-baptized also request to be immersed. Since baptism is not repeatable, and since remembering one's baptism is not as important as remembering the accepting of personal responsibility through church membership vows for what the Church and the home accepted at a child's baptism, and in view of the fact that baptism with water is not limited to baptism under water, nor is water baptism the primary baptism, but Spirit baptism is maybe pastors need to teach Christian church members that regeneration or the new birth is basic and critical and baptism is a sign of the change that has created the new creation (II Cor. 5:17).

The unrepeatability of baptism is based on the confession of churches that there is "one baptism" (Eph. 4:5), and in the life of any one individual baptism is a unique and unrepeatable act.[24]

The error in much that is said regarding water baptism is to be found in where baptism is rooted. That is, it is rooted in the water in which a person is buried. When in fact it ought to be "rooted in the ministry of Jesus of Nazareth, in his death and in his resurrection."[25]

Rooting baptism in Jesus of Nazareth implies that it is both a point of beginning for Christians as members of the body of Christ, in that through baptism they are incorporated into his body, and baptism relates Christians to a life-long growth process, through which they grow up into the daily beauty of Christ (II Cor. 3:18).

Baptism into the death and resurrection is linked with the receiving of the Spirit. The particular action or actions, whether one or all, including the water rite, the anointing with chrism, and/or the imposition of hands have been associated as the sign of the gift of the Spirit. The gift may be associated with one or all three actions according to various church bodies but all churches agree "the Christian baptism is in water and the Holy Spirit."[26]

What does baptism do? Possibly, a better way of stating the question is: What does God effect through baptism? Earlier, following the lead of J. S. Whale it was implied that baptism as a sign "effects something. It conveys what it signifies." By virtue of baptism being one of the two sacraments it is a rite in which God comes to us. "The heart of the Sacrament is divine action."[27] The action in baptism is the washing, or the cleansing. It is the sign through which public testimony is given to the truth. "The blood of Jesus his Son cleanses us from all sin" (I John 1:7).

In the Letter to the Ephesians this theme is addressed. "... Christ loved the church and gave himself up for her, that he might sanctify her, having cleansed her by the washing of water with the word" (Eph. 5:25, 26). The word refers to the formula used over the candidate. "In the name of the Father, and of the Son, and of the Holy Ghost" (Matt. 28:19). It has to do with Christ as the minister of baptism: "You are already made clean by the word which

I have spoken to you'' (John 15:3). The idea is that a corporate baptism of the church has taken place with Christ as the minister. And at the baptism of each person that corporate baptism of the church which stands as though it is a background is also the community into which each person is incorporated. Baptism in a sense is the rite of passage into that community which existed before the baptism of any believer. It admits believers into ''fellowship with us,'' to use John s words, ''and our fellowship is with the Father and with his Son Jesus Christ'' (I John 1:3).

John Wesley addressing this issue wrote that ''By baptism we are admitted into the Church, and consequently made members of Christ, its Head ... From which spiritual, vital union with him, proceeds the influence of his grace on those that are baptized; as from our union with the Church, a share in all its privileges, and in all its the promises Christ has made to it''.[28]

HOLY COMMUNION

1. **Will you say a few words on the different names by which this sacrament is called?**

It might be misleading to make too much of names used in references to the sacrament of Holy Communion in that for many of us we use them interchangeably. The word ''Eucharist'', or ''the Thanksgiving ... is its most primitive name and puts the emphasis where the early Church did.''[29] So the word ''Eucharist'' emphasizes the Thanksgiving on behalf of the Christian Church as it participates by word and action in the sacrament.

The words "Holy Communion" come down on the side of the sacred or the special or that which God has set apart as His means of communicating with His people. Communion denotes a fellowship and a relationship of a unique nature. In the Holy Communion Christ is present with us in the breaking of the bread and in the sharing of the cup (I Cor. 10:16).

"The Lord's Supper" emphasizes the meal aspect which also picks up the theme of the community of the faithful gathered as guests at the table of the Lord, who is also the host. Partaking of the bread and the fruit of the vine the guests fulfill what is required. For as Jesus said, "Except ye eat the flesh of the Son of man, and drink his blood, ye have no life in you. Whoso eateth my flesh, and drinketh my blood, hath eternal life; ..." (John 6:54-55).

2. **Will you discuss the Lord's Supper in light of the Articles of Religion?**

Yes, this discussion will be centered in Articles 18 and 19 of the 25 Articles of Religion.[30] Article 18 reads, thusly

> "The Supper of the Lord is not only a sign of the love that Christians ought to have among themselves one to another, but rather is a sacrament of our redemption by Christ's death; insomuch that, to such as rightly, worthily, and with faith receive the same, the bread which we break is a partaking of the body of Christ; and likewise the cup of blessing is a partaking of the blood of Christ.
>
> Transubstantiation, or the change of the substance of bread and wine in the Supper of the Lord can not be proved by Holy Writ; but is repugnant to the plain words of Scripture,

overthroweth the nature of a sacrament, and hath given occasion to many superstitions.

The body of Christ is given, taken, and eaten in the Supper, only after an heavenly and spiritual manner. And the means whereby the body of Christ is received and eaten in the Supper, is faith.

The Sacrament of the Lord's Supper was not Christ's ordinance reserved, carried about, lifted up, or worshipped.''

And Article 19 states

''The cup of the Lord is not to be denied to the lay people: for both parts of the Lord's Supper, by Christ's ordinance and commandments, ought to be administered to all Christians alike.''

Let us go back to Articles 18 and look at its meaning. First, the Article states that the Lord's Supper is a sign of love. But, note that the sign of love moves down to an ethical love. That is, it is love that Christians ought to have one for another. The meaning here is that undergirding the sacrament of the Lord's Supper is the unselfish love of God toward us as exemplified in the crucifixion of Jesus on the Cross. That kind of love ought to exist in the interactions and relationships between Christians.

Second, the Lord's Supper is the outward sign of our redemption. Our redemption, that is, our being bought back from sin and death, is the work of Christ's death. Again, the Crucifixion of Jesus is the key to the meaning of this sacrament.

Third, the Article sets forth three words as the conditions for taking the sacrament. One, the word ''rightly''; two, the word ''worthily''; and, three, the word ''faith.'' These three words are not defined as to their meanings. However, we are not without help in this regard. Such is so because we issue "the Invitation To Commune" and the Invitation spells out the condition.

As we know, there are five motifs in the invitation. They are, one, repentance; two, in love with the neighbor; three, intention, that is, intend to lead a new life; four, walking, that is, in the holy ways of God; and, five, drawing or coming to the sacrament with faith.

Repentance in religious circles means a change of direction. But before a person can be expected to change direction, there must be a sense of going the wrong way. In other words, there must be a feeling of guilt and remorse or godly sorrow for the way one is living. Immanuel Kant wrote about what he called "the categorical imperative." Which interpreted means, as he said, "There are just two things that fill me with awe, the starry sky above and the moral law within." The moral law within is the something, call it conscience, which says "you ought or ought not." This moral law is the gadfly in the soul that moves one to a change of direction.

Let us move now to "Ye that ... are in love and charity with your neighbor." Jesus highlighted the importance of loving relationships when he said in Matthew 5:23-23

> "So if you are about to offer your gift to God at the altar and there you remember that your brother has something against you, leave your gift there in front of the altar and go at once to make peace with your brother; then come back and offer your gift to God." (GNB).

The Lord's Supper is one of the means of grace that is implied in the General Rules of our church. But, what in love and charity with your neighbor means is that an individual cannot have a good relationship with God, a divine-human relationship, apart from a good human with human relationship. Therefore, if this means of grace is to be effective those who participate in the Lord's Supper must have the human-with-human relationship in order.

We go now to "Intend to lead a new life." Repentance is the new direction motif, but it relates significantly to the past. Intention points forward, to the future. It is a kind of blueprint. The specific thing a communicant intends to do is: "to lead a new life." In so many words because these words are given each time Holy Communion is served there is in them the recognition that communicants have not reached perfection but are constantly called to fulfill the command of Jesus, "Be ye perfect" and they remind us of the Methodist saying, "Going on to perfection." Consequently, there is no stopping place in this life for Christians. The Christian life leads onward and upward, one must ever press on the upward way, gaining new spiritual heights everyday.

Fourthly, there is the walking aspect. The person who intends to lead a new life finds it in the ways of God. In the Bible, "Ways" refers to "paths" - "the paths of the Lord." In Second Samuel "The way of the Lord is perfect." And the first psalms ends with the words, "The way of the ungodly shall perish." John the Baptist preached, saying, "Prepare ye the way of the Lord."

"Walking from henceforth in his holy ways" implies going from this place to that place. It suggests movement but it suggests also the nature of doing for ways point to a philosophy of life. With going, then, the way of doing as we go must be in keeping with the will and way of God. And His will and way point to loving redemptively.

Lastly, the words, "Draw near with faith." Holy Communion becomes in the presence of faith or to faith participation in the body and blood of Christ. Faith is a kind of receptacle, a receiver of the very grace that gave it existence. In the process of grace and faith intermingling; the death of Jesus, the Christ of God, is more than a memory of a past event. What was is, the past is made present, and the past that is made present is efficacious, effective in the now. Jesus who died on Calvary is Christ present as a heavenly, spiritual reality. At the table, Christ is present, alive, and, the means of his living presence, bread and fruit of the vine, keep him consciously before his Church until he comes again at the end.

3. **In which directions does Holy Communion point?**

Most people that I have talked with over the years seem to understand that the Lord's Supper though instituted by Jesus on the Thursday before his crucifixion on Friday rests upon and is dependent for its meaning on the crucifixion of Jesus of Nazareth.

Of course a lot of meaning is lost if the only *Look is Past* in the celebration of the Lord's Supper. The Sacrament is a memorial that is done in remembrance of Jesus the Christ (Luke 22:19b). But remembrance of the past demands a *Look in the Present*. Jesus Christ who finished the work of redemption on Calvary's Cross is present with those who do this in remembrance of him. And the Christ who is present is also the subject of the *Look to the Future*, when he comes at the end time in glory.

But, how is he present? Look first at what he said to his disciples on that Thursday night in the Upper

Room. "This is my body which is given for you" (Luke 22:19) and "This cup which is poured out for you is the new covenant in my blood" (Luke 22:20). The bread that he broke "is my body" and the cup that he took after supper "is the new covenant in my blood."

The bread and the cup are the vessels which bear the presence of Jesus the Christ. The Christian Church has the given, the datum, the fact of the promise of Jesus to be present "where two or three are gathered in my name" (Matt. 18:20). Having his promise and in as much as the Lord is not slow about his promise (II Pet. 3:9) the real issue ought not be his presence. Instead the issue now ought to be that since he is present the Church gathered to share his presence in the Sacrament of Holy Communion should express in life and witness the communion and fellowship they have together in Christ. Paul put the matter in order in his Letter to the Church at Galatia when he wrote, "If we live by the Spirit, let us also walk by the Spirit" (Gal. 5:25). Living by the Spirit is the description of being controlled by God and "to walk by the Spirit" is the description of proper attitude and behavior of a Christian. Paul said, "Let us have no self conceit, no provoking of one another, no envy of one another" (Gal. 5:26).

The encounter that Christians have with Christ in the Sacrament of Holy Communion is God coming to us as we *re-call* or *re-present* an event before Him. This is what remembrance means. Paul raised the questions of the real presence of Christ in communal terms. He asked the Corinthians: "The cup of blessing which we bless, is it not a participation in the blood of Christ? The bread which we break, is it not a participation in the body of Christ?" (I Cor. 10:16).

4. **How do we experience Christ in the Sacrament?**

Is individual participation in the blood of Christ automatic? That is, though Christ be present is anything required of the participant in order to experience Christ? Holy Communion is not spiritual medicine that works without faith. To be sure the redemptive work of Christ which stands behind and empowers the Sacrament is *there*, it is historical fact. And in the action of "Taking" and "Blessing" and "Breaking" and "Sharing" the Christ-event is RE-PRESENTED before God who is gathered with His people, the body of Christ. And in the company of the worshipping community by remembering Christ the PAST is PRESENT and the FUTURE realized. Paul said it well, "For as often as you eat this bread and drink the cup, you proclaim the Lord's death until he comes" (1 Cor. 11:26).

In the Lord's Supper Christ is present *to faith*. Let us keep in mind that the gathering together of the Church is an act of faith. The gathering symbolizes faith in the promise of Jesus to be present. And when they are gathered in his name Christ is there. He is "Present to the faith of the receiver" of the elements of Holy Communion in what D.M. Baillie called a *more real* way "because this presence is more penetrating than any merely local or spatial presence could be".[31]

In the Lord's Supper there is as Baillie pointed out "The Presence, The Memory And The Hope." In the Sacrament Christ is present in his body, the Church, to faith. But as was alluded to earlier his presence as memory or re-presentation is not all there is. "Until he comes" places the Church in the realm of hope. Just as celebrating Holy Communion is re-presenting Calvary, this proclamation is keeping the future alive in the present. The redeemed proclaim the Lord's death until he comes.

Jurgen Moltmann wrote, saying

> Christ is our hope because Christ is our future. That means that we are waiting and hoping for his second coming, praying 'Come, Lord Jesus, come to the world, come to us!' Just as the resurrection faith is hope's foundation, so Christ's second coming defines hope's horizon. Without the expectation of Christ's second coming there is no Christian hope, for without it hope is not putting its trust in a radical alternative to this world's present condition.[32]

THE CHURCH

1. **Will you expand on the meaning and nature of the church?**

I suppose a good place to start is with the Source and the Foundation of the Church. It is of *God*. He founded it upon "the blood of his own Son" (Acts 20:28). Christ is the head and the Church is his body (Col. 1:18). By grace through faith (Eph. 2:8-9) the members of the body are saved and by baptism they put on Christ (Gal. 3:27).

The Church is *one*. In spite of the many members of the body, the body is one. God the Source is One (Gal. 3:20). Christ the head is not divided, thus, he is one (I Cor. 1:13). He is the one, the *one-ly* mediator between God and human beings (I Tim. 2:5). As the one undivided Head of the one body and the one-ly mediator through whom God works reconciliation he is also the one way through which entry into the body is possible. (John 10:7-18)

The Church is *apostolic*. It is not a fly-by-night institution. It traces its history back to those who were known of Jesus and who came to know him. What is preached and taught have come from them.

The apostle John put it thus:

> "That which was from the beginning, which we have heard, which we have seen with our eyes, which we have looked upon and touched with our hands, concerning the word of life—the life was made manifest, and we saw it, and testify to it, and proclaim to you the eternal life which was with the Father and was made manifest to us—that which we have seen and heard we proclaim also to you so that you may have fellowship with us, and our fellowship is with the Father and with his Son Jesus Christ. And we are writing this that our joy may be complete." (I John 1:1-4)

The Church is *catholic*. I like to think that its catholic nature is because of Christ. The Gospel according to John explained God giving His only Son with the words, "For God so loved the world" (John 3:16). For John at least God's purpose and plan was universal. Or, it was catholic. Paul's letter to the Church at Colossae presents Christ as the one for whom all things were created "in heaven and on earth" and he is the one through whom God sought "to reconcile to himself all things, whether on earth or in heaven, making peace by the blood of his cross" (Col. 1:20).

Christ is thus the agency of creation and he is also the agent of reconciliation for the universe. The church represents those in the world who with Christ "died to the elemental spirits of the universe" (Col. 2:20). It is the community of those who "have been raised with Christ" and now "seek the things that are above, where Christ is, seated at the right hand of God" (Col. 3:1). As the community increases the world decreases. In the letter to the Colossians this concept seems to be the way in which the universal redemption of Christ becomes actual. So the catholic church or the universal church is rooted in Christ as the individed Savior (I Cor. 1:13) of the whole world whose body is also one (Rom. 12:4-5).

The catholicity of the church is represented, I believe, by the fellowship aspect. There exists a community of believers who are bonded together through faith in Jesus as the Savior and Lord of life and exis tence. This community goes beyond denominations while at the same time it exists within them.

2. **From the several "official documents" of our church what positions on the church are expressed?**

The position of the Articles of Religion on the church expresses itself in several aspects. One, it calls this entity "The visible Church of Christ." That would have to be seen in contrast with the so called "invisible Church," which stresses the spiritual relationship of individuals with Christ. It is on this relationship that fellowship is founded and rests.

Two, it is "a congregation of faithful men." The Church is the congregation that is characterized by faithfulness to Christ. Three, in this congregation "the pure word of God is preached, and the sacraments duly administered." Which suggests that the church gathered or the church as the worshipping community is emphasized.[33]

The Constitution of the C.M.E. Church describes the church first, as of God; second, existing to the end of time; third, it exists for, one, to promote worship; two, to administer preaching and the sacraments; three, to maintain Christian fellowship and discipline; four, to edify or to build up believers in Christ; five, to convert the world; and six, to transform the structures of society so that the things in society that prevent and deny human beings the right to be human and to mature in their humanity may be changed and altered and amended.[34]

Our Constitution also goes back and picks up the Article of Religion and says "This is a visible Church of Christ, consisting of faithful persons, in which the pure Word of God is preached and the Sacraments duly administered."[35] What is called "a congregation" in Article of Religion 13 is extended to a "connection". As the Church of Christ was localized it is herein connectionalized. But the connection must be understood as expressed in every local congregation. So that what is local in the Articles of Religion is not altered in the Constitution. In that the connection as "a visible Church of Christ" is expressed in its many units or local churches. But, I must also make it clear that when the Constitution makes the claim that "This is a visible Church of Christ" it means also that its local congregations are one by one "The visible Church of Christ." And in a real sense the Church expressed connectionally is the sum of its many congregations.

3. **What is the job or the mission of the church?**

In discussing the meaning and nature of the church, I brought the answer to this question into the discussion. So what is said here may be a repeat but I hope it will also expand on what was previously stated.

The pilgrim people is God's people living between the times. Those who once were "no people but now you are God's people" (I Pet. 2:10) exist as the body of Christ between the times of his ascension (Acts 1:9) and the time of his return (Acts 1:10-11).

The first thing the people of God, the body of Christ, are to do is *to be the Church*. Its life is to manifest as mind and spirit the attitudinal posture of its Christ. ''Have this mind among yourselves, which is yours in Christ Jesus'' (Philip. 2:5). He did not try to become like God (Philip. 2:6; SEE, Gen. 3:5). He became the servant of God and of humanity (Philip. 2:7-8). God exalted him to a place of singular honor (Philip. 2:9-11).

This means that it is the job or the vocation or the function of the Church to manifest in its institutional life genuine fellowship. Love among members of the body ought be a primal witness to the world that they are disciples of Christ (John 13:35). In the visible assemblies of God's people the fulness of the Spirit of Christ must abide.

All things that are held in common by God's people must be shared in community in a spirit of fellowship. ''There is one body, and one Spirit, just as you were called to the one hope that belongs to your call, one Lord, one faith, one baptism, one God and Father of us all and through all and in all'' (Eph. 4:4-6).

It is the job of the Church to lead the kind of life that enhances ''the unity of the Spirit in the bond of peace'' (Eph. 4:3). Such requires ''lowliness and meekness, with patience, forbearing one another in love'' (Eph. 4:2).

The visible fellowship ought be a token of the unity of the spirit between Jesus and the Father.

The fellowship as the visible assembly of the saints is the context of worship (Matt. 18:20). It is the place of edification of the two or three who gather together in the name of Jesus.''Let all things be done for edification'' (I Cor. 14:26d).

Every gift given by Christ to the Church is given ''to equip the saints for the work of ministry, for building up of the body of Christ'' (Eph. 4:12). The spiritual health of the fellowship is a concern of critical importance. Its job is to help a pilgrim people to reach ''the measure of the stature of Christ'' (Eph. 4:13b). It functions best when it is one, when its message is built upon the teaching of the apostles, when its spirit and world view is universal and inclusive, and when it recognizes its own sinful tendencies which make it forever in need of reform by the Spirit.

The mission or the job of the Church is to *proclaim the Gospel*. The whole church ''built upon the foundation of the apostles and prophets, Christ Jesus himself being the cornerstone'' (Eph. 2:20) ''is a chosen race, a royal priesthood, a holy nation, God's own people'' (I Pet. 2:9).

The privileged position of those who are in Christ and who make up the one body of Christ (I Cor. 12:14) have the responsibility of proclaiming his good news. They have been called out of the world, equipped, and sent into the world to ''declare the wonderful deeds of him who called you out of darkness into his marvelous light'' (I Pet. 2:9b).

Proclamation is the Word preached, and through the hearing of the preaching of Christ faith is made alive (Rom. 10:17). Proclamation is the Word celebrated in the Lord's Supper (I Cor. 10:16). In the spoken Word and in the Word acted Christ is present.

The fellowship gathered together in the name of Jesus assemble around Jesus Christ who is present in his Word by the Holy Spirit. No matter the manner in which the story of the Word is presented in the fellowship, by sermon or by sacrament, it proposes to "make bodily growth" (Eph. 4:16d), which is the nurturing ministry of the Church and its equipping ministry.

In order for upbuilding in love to be complete the visible body has the authority to discipline. It is empowered with authority to discipline and to ex-communicate (Matt. 18:15-18). The spiritual character of the Church as the called out ones must be strengthened and when a member will not be reproved, the Church has the authority to discipline.

Lastly, *the Church is in the world to serve.* "The deeds of him who called" the Church into being constitute the summary of God's saving and liberating activity in the world. Christ in whom God was reconciling the world unto Himself (II Cor. 5:19) assumed and lived out the ministry of the Servant of God and the servant of humanity.

In the synagogue in Nazareth, Jesus cast his mission in terms written by the prophet Isaiah. He took the book and read, saying, he had come to "preach good news to the poor," to "proclaim release to the captives and the recovering of sight to the blind, to set at liberty those who are oppressed, to proclaim the acceptable year of the Lord" (Luke 4:18f, Isa. 61:1).

The Church as the reconciled (token) and reconciling (instrument) community of God's love has as its mission the mission of its Lord. It is to be God's servant in the world to "complete what remains of Christ's affliction for the sake of the body, that is, the church" (Col. 1:24).

Service takes several shapes in ministry: waiting tables; caring for the bodily needs of others (SEE.

Luke 8:3; Mk. 15:41, Matt. 24:45) and certain acts of love that may be special (Matt. 25:42-44).

Service means fundamentally "living for others." The Church as the community of the redeemed, the fellowship of the reconciled lives for others through the ministry of reconciliation.

To what extend and to what limits does service reach? It extends to wherever there is the disjointed, or where there is a chasm, a gulf, or a barrier which deny one person or many the opportunity to grow up into the fullness of God's intention and plan for His creation.

Where some in the creation are yet waiting because of injustices to be set free from bondage and obtain the full liberty of the children of God (cf. Rom. 8:18-23) the Church must address by Word and action the consciousness crystalized in systems and structures; and where persons of power deny others their liberty, the people of God must be prophetic in word and deed.

LIFE, DEATH AND ETERNITY

1. What is our belief about human life?

It is clear from our official documents that we hold to a view of human life as sacred. Not-with-standing the doctrine of original sin as "the corruption of the nature of every man" we hold that "each person is of infinite worth, and a child of God."[36] Since sex is regarded biblically as the most intimate form of knowing between two persons our view that marriage is the proper context for sexual expression is illuminating relative to our view on human life.[37] Likewise, just as sexual exploitation profanes the sacred, denial of certain God given inalienable rights "because of race, creed, culture, national origin or social class" is an offense to God who "out of one blood ... made all the nations to dwell on the face of the earth."

Because human life is sacred the church is in the world "to serve and save society".[38] The sacred-ness of human life is due to its relation to God. The human being is *some-body* because God is mindful of him or her (Ps. 8:4). We are because God is. "In him we live and move and have our being" (Acts 27:28).

2. **What do we believe about death?**

What we believe about death is determined in large measure by what we believe about life. Which fact paves the way for me to expand on what we believe about life. My use of the words "what we believe" is not intended to imply that what I write is the official interpretation of this denomination. Rather, my reference is often to positions widely and generally held by Protestant churches that look to the Bible and to scholarly interpreters for guidance in their interpretation of Christian doctrine.

Let us take a look at the meaning of human life. J. Robert Nelson has written that "Human life according to biblical thinking is monistic, unitary. It is the concrete existence of the whole human being. Rather than connoting an invisible, timeless soul which temporarily inhabits a mortal organism, life means temporality, spatiality, mobility, self-direction."[39]

The *living* God in the Bible also "*makes alive.* Adam did not *receive* a living soul, or *nepes*; he *became* a living soul."[40] By the providence of God nurturing and sustaining the life He made that life has value and vitality both actually and potentially in relation to the meaning of its existence.

"Life as a loan from God," to use Professor Nelson's word may be defined by the well known words "quality of life." Such life is "defined and measured ... by the living out day by day of the Creator's expectations, which are intensely moral. Life is not only holistic in the sense of being the integration of the whole person; it is also holy because its deepest meaning consists of being in accord with the Creator's purpose."[41]

So the one God idea of the Old Testament leads to the idea of one life and to the position that "man is an indivisible whole which may be seen from various points of view such as flesh, body, soul, spirit, or heart."[42]

In subscribing to the Hebraic ideas we must be careful not to give in to Greek influence. The Jewish thought forms are concrete and whole whereas the thought forms of the Greeks are abstract and departmentalized. So, then, we should not be misled into dividing up the human being on the basis of Jesus having said, "You shall love the Lord your God with all your heart, and with all your soul, and with all your mind" (Matt. 22:37). He was emphasizing the demand of total commitment to God of the whole person. And by the same token any one of the several aspects represented the whole. So by enumerating the parts and placing each under the command Jesus should not be misunderstood in his demanding total and complete love of God.

The human being who becomes a living soul by God's love and nurture lives a quality oriented life according to the Christian point of view when he or she links up with Jesus who "came that they may have life, and have it abundantly'' (John 10:10b). And because a person lives unto Christ he or she dies ''with dignity.'' Living and dying are ''to the Lord.'' ''For to this end Christ died and lived again, that he might be Lord both of the dead and of the living'' (Rom. 14:9).

Those who die in the Lord are called ''blessed'' (Rev. 14:13) because of Christ. As we live in hope we die in hope (I Cor. 15:19). Also, as life is one and as the human being ''Is a psychophysical unit''[43] that human unit lives ''three dimensions at once. the bodily life of the flesh, the psychic and moral life of the soul, and the fulfilled and resurrected life of the complete person.''[44] All three are lived ''with undifferentiated attribution to God.''

Death spells the end of life. Kantonen quoted Epicurus who said, ''When we are, death is not, and when death is, we are not.''[45] ''Death is a major event.'' ... ''It is the hour at which our whole earthly record stands closed''.[46] Let it be clear that ''Man does not have a mortal part, the body, and an immortal part, the soul. He is an indivisible unit, a body-animated-by-soul. As such, whether viewed under the body-aspect or the soul-aspect, he exists solely by his relation to God. Death is the breach of this relationship.''[47]

Put succinctly, in death the whole person dies. So the unitary nature of human beings is a denial of an immortal soul that escapes death and the grave by leaving the body and going back to where it came from. Jesus, we affirm in the Apostles' Creed, was ''crucified ..., dead ... and buried ...'' Each of us dies, also; our total being dies.

3. **What is meant by the biblical words of Jesus, "Father, into thy hands I commit my spirit"? (Luke 23:46) Or, the earlier words, "and the spirit returns to God who gave it"? (Eccl. 11:7b).**

Persons who understand the original language of the Bible have shown that the Hebrew word *ruah* is usually translated "spirit" or "breath". "Its root meaning is like that of the Greek *pneuma-* the wind or the breath."[48] When the word is related to life (hayyim) it denotes "the breath of life" and "signifies man's source in God"[49] upon whom we are dependent for the "continuity of being alive" and "the breath of life" which is His loan to us "sustains life's duration in time, and when it ceases the whole creature is dead."[50]

What Jesus committed to the Father and what returns to Him at death is "the breath of life." God who gives the breath of life which provides us with the capacity "to become a living being" (Gen. 2:7b) is Spirit and to Him spirit rightly returns. When the spirit returns to God, James wrote that "the body apart from the spirit is dead" (Jas. 2:26). It is the life principle and is not the soul.

4. **Now, will you say something about the meaning of "soul"?**

One of the best explanations for the word "soul" is a common use made of it. It is common to hear a person say, "Five souls were saved during our revival." Now they do not mean souls without bodies were saved. The reference is to five persons with names and histories and each is identified and recognized by certain physical attributes as seen in a body and each may upon close examination reveal certain peculiar characteristics that are "spiritual" or inner.

The body is soul-animated. "The body is the soul in its outward form" (Pederson).[51] The soul is not an attachment to the body, nor is it an appendage, neither is it an insert added at some particular time. Instead, soul (Psyche) "stands for life." "For what will it profit a man, if he gains the whole world and forfeits his *life*" (Matt. 16:26). The soul is inseparable from the body.[52] When the life of an individual reflects quality and nobility in the flesh and makes us say of an individual "What a beautiful soul" we have an awareness of what soul means in the Bible.

The soul dies with our death.

5. **What do we believe about "the resurrection of the body"?**

Let me remind us of what we do not affirm in the Apostles Creed. We do not say "I believe in the immortality of the soul." Yet when it is written that we say instead, "I believe in ... the resurrection of the body," we somehow think they are the same. For that reason as well as for the sake of being true to the faith, I have stressed that death brings the whole of a person to its end. The soul does not fly away. We die completely, wholly.

The resurrection of the dead is related to the resurrection of Christ. As I stated earlier we affirm that he was crucified until he was dead. It was critical to the early church Fathers that "dead" was emphasized, because there were those who taught that Jesus "seemed to die." Thus, the apologists or defenders of the faith were careful to show that Jesus really and truly died.

He was raised from the dead (Acts 4:10) in bodily form. The fact that there was apparent continuity and discontinuity with his pre-burial appearance may indeed give more rather than less support to Paul's claim that with the resurrection to come "God gives it a body as he has chosen" (I Cor. 15:38).

The resurrected Jesus was seen by Mary yet John reported "she did not know it was Jesus" (John 20:14). Yet, when Jesus called her, saying, "Mary" she responded saying, "Rab-bo-ni" (which means Teacher) (John 20:16). The resurrection of Christ is the cornerstone of the Christian religion. And the matter of personal continuity while it may not be in bodily form or appearance, evidently from the experiences individuals had with the resurrected Jesus, does exist. Not only did Mary not recognize Jesus neither did the disciples walking on the Emmaus Road. It was in breaking bread with them after they reached the village that "their eyes were opened and they recognized him" (Luke 24:31). On the one hand he entered through locked doors (John 20:19) and on the other he showed "his hands and side" (John 20:20) as marks of his identity. There was both a carryover from the pre-crucifixion life and there was something new.

So there would seem to be the same in our understanding of the meaning of "the resurrection of the body." For it is more than the negative response to the Greek idea of the immortality of the soul. The belief is in the power of God to create something new. With Paul we can say this much, "It is sown a physical body, it is raised a spiritual body. If there is a physical body, there is also a spiritual body" (I Cor. 15:44).

Merrill R. Abbey maintained that "Believing in the resurrection of the body, we do not believe in the resuscitation of the flesh but in the continued identity of the person."[53] Oscar Cullmann called it "a new act of creation which embraces everything, it is not an event which begins with each individual death, but only at the *End.*''[54] The identity that is continued is not ''flesh and blood'' which ''cannot inherit the kingdom'' (I Cor. 15:50). Identity is in the creation that God brings in calling ''back to life not just a part of the man, but the whole man—all that God had created and death had annihilated.''[55] Belief in the immortality of the soul does not require faith in the grace of God to keep us in death and to resurrect the body in the End. Death the last enemy of God from which Jesus took the sting (I Cor. 15:54) has no apparent power over the soul for those who believe in its immortality. Such is not what belief in ''the resurrection of the body'' means. It means that death is real and powerful and in the flesh ''all die'' (I Cor. 15:22). And ''Resurrection is a *positive* assertion: the whole man, who has really died, is recalled to life by a new act of creation by God.''[56]

6. **Does it really matter whether we believe in ''the immortality of the soul'' or ''the resurrection of the body''?**

I think that anyone who belongs to a C.M.E. Church has made a choice. In that light it matters whether or not a member seeks to understand the choice that has been made, which is for ''the resurrection of the body''. Such understanding ought to move an individual toward an appreciation for a significant event, the resurrection, that has the capacity to heighten personal faith in God. Immortality of the soul is without such capacity, for it is ''a passive assertion''. It requires no faith because it is, supposedly, automatic.

The choice you make makes a difference because it seems to me that it means being or not being on the side of New Testament evidence. The evidence of the New Testament is that a human being really and completely dies. There is no indestructible part called the soul. Every part of a human being withers into non-being before the wind of death. The reality of death as decisive upon the life and existence of a human being is important if the victory of Jesus over sin and death is to have ultimate meaning. In contrast to Socrates who welcomed death in order that his soul might be freed from its prison, which was the body of Socrates, Jesus was troubled (Mark 15:34, 37., Mark 14:33).[57] It was by confronting the power of evil and triumphing over its twin expressions sin and death by dying and being raised from the dead that death lost its sting and the grave was denied its power to hold. Had there been a soul in need of release from the body Jesus could have died without anxiety and anguish. Rather, when his life was about to be snuffed out he recoiled and it was afterwards that he moved to accept the will of the Father. Still, while on the cross he cried under death's burden, "My God, my God, why hast thou forsaken me?" (Matt. 27:46). Death cast its spell of darkness and isolation and loneliness upon him. It was not a thing of beauty. But an awe-ful event and its might caused Jesus to feel deserted.

Cast against the background of a real death the resurrection of Christ means "that the whole person of Jesus was raised from death to a wholly new order or dimension of life."[58] Upon his resurrection "hinges the whole Christian message and the whole Christian hope."[59] His resurrection is the empowerment of our resurrection. ''By a man has come also the resurrection from the dead'' (I Cor. 15:21). And in this one man, Christ, ''shall all be made alive'' (I Cor. 15:22).

The resurrection of the dead is a belief set upon faith in God and it is rooted in Christ as our hope. It is our belief that God in Christ has given us the victory over ''the sting of death'' (I Cor. 15:56, 57). And though it is appointed for us to die once (Heb. 9:27) not even death shall ''separate us from the love of God in Christ Jesus our Lord'' (Rom. 8:39). The Christ of God who ''has been raised from the dead'' (I Cor. 15:20) is also the one in whom our life is hid and ''When Christ who is our life appears, then you will also appear with him in glory'' (Col. 3:4). He is our life, thus, our hope. As such our future does not reside in anything that is in us but it rests in Christ ''the hope of glory'' (Col. 11:27c). God who did not leave Christ in the grave can be trusted to raise us up.

7. **What do we believe about ''the life everlasting''? And, how does this fit into ''the resurrection of the body'' concept, which is, you said, a *new* creation?**

It is my conviction that belief in the life everlasting is in tune with belief in the resurrection of the body. The primary thing to keep in mind is that according to Jesus he came that we might have *life* (John 10:10). The next point is this: Jesus claimed to be *the life* (John 14:6). The third point is this, Jesus said that eternal or everlasting life is in knowing the only true God and in knowing Jesus Christ whom the one true God sent to bring the abundant life to the world (John 17:3).

Knowing God through Jesus Christ is not a matter of information. Knowing God does not mean that we have learned from Jesus some very interesting things about God. Knowing God is intimate because Jesus revealed God. He did not come as one who brought loads of helpful information about God. From the outset it was said of Jesus by an angel speaking to Joseph, "his name shall be called Emmanuel" (which means God with us) (Matt. 1:23b). And Jesus flatly said to Philip, one of his disciples, "He who has seen me has seen the Father" (John 14:9). So it is not information that Jesus revealed. He revealed God Himself. And knowing God in Jesus of Nazareth required more than physical senses and physical encounters. Philip had those yet he asked Jesus to "show us the Father and we shall be satisfied" (John 14:8). Knowing was the result of trust and of belief. Jesus told his disciples to believe him, that is, accept the truth on the merit that he said "I am in the Father and the Father in me." But if they could not accept it as true by taking his word, then, "believe me for the sake of the works themselves" (John 14:11). He appealed to them to accept his works as signs of God's authority and rule in the world.

Jesus told his disciples in this same dialogue that trust and belief and the knowing that followed were the results of love. They must love him to be loved by the Father and whoever loves Jesus he said "I will love him and manifest myself to him" (John 14:21). So knowing is a matter of Jesus manifesting himself and that takes place within a relationship of love. Knowing is an intimate relationship between God and us with Jesus as the token and the instrument.

How does this little discussion fit into everlasting life as a belief? We know God through Jesus the Christ in whom God was reconciling the world to Himself (II Cor. 5:19). We know Jesus as the Christ by faith and that knowledge makes us new creatures (II Cor. 5:16-17). Further, as we come to know Jesus as the Christ and to know him as God's Anointed or the Christ of God we become His children by grace through faith (Gal. 3:25-27). The saved are in Christ who is seated at the right hand of the Father. What the saved have that is unique is a life giving and life sustaining relationship with God through Jesus the Christ. This relationship begins in this life with knowing God in His Christ. Life everlasting is quality of life that comes to us as a gift through God's only Son who lived the abundant life. Which is life lived according to the way God intended human beings to live.

Because we are mortal and sinful and because the world is also an imperfect place, eternal life is incomplete here, but it cannot be destroyed by death. That because it is in Christ and its everlasting quality is not with us. He keeps it. God vouchsafed it to him. And when we have been raised from death in the body which God will give Paul's "then" in this saying will be fulfilled. "For now we see in a mirror dimly, but then face to face. Now I know in part; then I shall understand fully, even as I have been fully understood" (I Cor. 13:12).

8. **When will "the resurrection of the body" and the next phase of "the life everlasting" take place?**

This question does not intend to imply that a date is meant when this will happen. Rather it is a question on sequences or phases. And it seems as Oscar Cullmann noted that this will occur as an Event in what might be called the "end-time."

I have shown in an earlier passage in this chapter that "the believer already has eternal life" but I share a quote from Cullmann which ties the *eternal life now* concept with the thought that even for the believer ''the raising of the body takes place only at the last day'' and the believer having the Spirit within knows that ''God *has* delivered us from death and *will* deliver us'' (II Cor. 1:22).[60]

As for as the time when ''the corruptible will put on the incorruptible'' Jesus took ''His stand against all calculations of the future'' by saying, ''But of that day or that hour no one knows, not even the angels in heaven, nor the Son, but only the Father'' (Mark 13:32).[61]

Biblically speaking, I believe we may say ''With the return of Christ the purpose of God for individual lives as well as for all history will achieve its ultimate end.''[62] The resurrection of Christ which both Paul (Rom. 1:4) and Peter (I Pet. 3:18) attributed to the power of the Holy Spirit effected in Jesus the change from flesh to spirit. So that which is our fulfillment, ''namely, the resurrection of bodies,'' and is now a reality in the resurrected Christ, ''will only happen at the end.''[63]

So the dead in Christ ''wait for the Lord Jesus Christ, who will conform our lowly body to the body of His glory'' (Philippians 3:21). When he returns and the resurrection of our bodies is brought about by the Holy Spirit we will have ''the means of life and expression'' of that which Merrill Abbey called the ''identity of the person,'' the personality.[64] No matter the state, whether dead or alive, ''we shall all be changed'' (I Cor. 15:51). And the transformation of the body takes place ''at the *End*, and this is to be understood literally, that is, in the temporal sense.''[65]

9. **Does the New Testament teach anything about where the dead are while they wait?**

"The condition of those who had died was not an object of primary concern to Christians in New Testament times.... Trust in Christ as the conqueror of death and giver of eternal life is central. Not death but the Risen Christ is the deliverer."[66]

For Cullmann there are leads nonetheless which help us in understanding something of the state of the dead. He held that in death the dead wait in what has been referred to as the "interim condition". As all who are in Christ have the Spirit of God dwelling in them in life so the dead have the Spirit in them (See: Rom. 8:11).

Paul referred to death as a condition of nakedness (II Cor. 5:1-4). He expressed also the idea of the anxiety of the inner man without a physical body. Anxiety may be overcome with the awareness that God "has given us the earnest of the Spirit" (II Cor. 5:5b). Thus, the dead who die in Christ are "in possession of the Holy Spirit." The Spirit as earnest keeps and holds us, so to speak, in death. In that sense the dead are not abandoned, they have the Holy Spirit. Because of the Spirit as earnest, "We are willing rather to be absent from the body, and to be at home with the Lord" (II Cor. 5:8).

The dead who "sleep" in the possession of the Holy Spirit are closer or nearer to Christ, they are "at home with the Lord." Death delivers us from the flesh, which is the main hinderance to our being filled with and of being in the possession of the Spirit. Once delivered by death, the person who was transformed in this life by the Holy Spirit is already grasped by the resurrection (Rom. 6:3ff, John 3:3ff), if he *has* already as a living person really been renewed by the

Holy Spirit. Although that individual still "sleeps" and still awaits the resurrection of the body which alone will give full life, the dead Christian *has* the Holy Spirit.[67]

The dead wait and those who sleep "in Christ" wait in the possession of the Holy Spirit. Not only is Christ our life while we live *in* time. He is our life *in* death. For that reason those who die in the Lord are called "blessed" or "happy" (Rev. 14:13). When Christ returns in the End the life that is yet incomplete for the dead will be made complete as the dead in Christ are raised and clothed in perfection.

Does this mean that since the dead in Christ have the Holy Spirit and the Spirit does not die that this interpretation is not different from belief in the immortality of the soul? There is a similarity to the extent that I have shown that there is continuity of life to some extent in both positions, either as a soul or as relationship. However, the position on the soul regards this part of persons as *essentially* immortal. So the soul which escapes or departs the human being at death may be assumed eternal. On the side of the dead in Christ being kept the claim is not based on anything that was necessary for the dead to live a natural life. That is, a person can live without ever confessing faith in Jesus the Christ. So the point here is that the Christian dead are in him of whom Paul wrote, saying, "For we know that Christ being raised from the dead will never die again; death no longer has dominion over him" (Rom. 6:9).

By dying as a creature of "flesh and blood" (Heb. 2:14) that "he might taste death for every one," (Heb. 2:9c), and by dying "destroy him who has the power of death, the devil," (Heb. 2:14b) Jesus liberated believers from "lifelong bondage" to the "fear of death" (Heb. 2:15). God's intention is to put all things in subjection to Christ including death. "As it is, we do not yet see everything in subjection to him. *But we see Jesus,* ..." (Heb. 2:8) (Emphasis added). Jesus, after having made "purification for sins, sat down at the right hand of the Majesty on high" (Heb. 1:3). He is the eternal one. Through "our Savior Christ Jesus" God "brought life and immortality to light through the gospel" (II Tim. 1:10). Immortality is Christ and those who die in him partake of this power over the dominion of death. Yet that which abides death is life and the Source of that life is the Spirit (II Cor. 3:6d). And in death the spirit returns to its Source who is eternal. What is promised in the resurrection is a new creation and not an old soul. At the place of interment "It is sown a physical body," and in the End, "it is raised a spiritual body" (II Cor. 15:44).

10. **What do we believe about the judgment?**

Belief in a final judgment means that we have already made a decision. Not everyone believes there is anything existing that will be judged. Karl Heim referred to that position as "the radical hopelessness of nihilism" and went on to describe it as the view "for which the whole course of the present world is merely an episode, which appears out of nothingness and disappears again into nothingness, leaving not a trace behind."[68]

In contrast to the idea of nothingness there is the position that creation has a Creator (Gen. 1:1). The Creator is God who made all things through the Word (John 1:3). By the power of God "the Word became flesh and dwelt among us, full of grace and truth" (John 1:14). In the Word a new era broke in upon history. So Christians celebrate what God has wrought in Christ's victorious triumph over sin, death, and the grave. Though we still celebrate his return to the Father as symbol of his finished work we live by faith between the time of his ascension and the time of his return. Thus, we do not subscribe to an idea that all life is vanity and all existence is futile, nor do we hold a position which regards history as recurring cycles; rather, we believe that while history is going somewhere more important is the fact that God's "eternal power has streamed into history from the cross; ... and ... that eternal power will outlast history."[69]

Thus, God in Christ invaded time as the New Dimension, the heavenly and the eternal, and transformed the whole system and those who are made new by faith in Christ "look not to the things that are seen but to the things that are unseen" (II Cor. 4:18a) and the reason why Christians are able to do so is because they are new creations, "the old has passed away, behold, the new has come" (II Cor. 5:17); thus, by the grace of God they now know that "the things that are seen are transient, but the things that are unseen are eternal" (II Cor. 4:18b).

God in Christ has already judged the world and exposed the "seen" or the "visible" as temporary and lacking the capacity to hold up and deliver security for human beings who long and thirst for "a spring of water welling up to eternal life" (John 4:14). John summarized the judgment, thus, "that the light has come into the world, and men loved darkness rather than light, because their deeds were evil" (John 3:19).

According to John, judgment is in human choices and the ultimate judgment is in the choice that human beings make for or against the One who matters ultimately. A hint of John's position is seen after Jesus announced that his soul was troubled due to his impending death on the cross (John 12:27, 32, 33). Anquished of soul he said, "Father, glorify thy name" (John 12:28a) and a voice answered from heaven saying, "I have glorified it, and I will glorify it again" (John 12:28b). Jesus told the confused crowd that the voice was for their sake and not his. Then, he talked on to let them know that the purpose of the voice was to make them aware of who he was, that he was indeed from God and he came that the Father through him might be made manifest in the world. His presence was judgment for "Now is the judgment of this world, now shall the ruler of this world be cast out, ..." (John 12:31). And having heard the Heavenly Voice the crowd was made aware by Jesus of his death on the cross and of his power to draw persons to him (John 12:32), but more to the point he told them of the urgency of making their decisions. He said, "the light is with you for a little longer" (John 12:35), and because of the possibility of being overtaken by the darkness (John 12:35b), he counseled, "While you have the light, believe in the light, that you may become sons of the light" (John 12:36).

In a very real sense the words of the Lord to Israel as spoken by Moses hold and present an eternal truth. His words capture and hold before us the truth that human beings are principal participants with God in the drama of human history, existence and life. As participants, and from the Christian side, we are first of all part of the world that God has judged in Christ. He is the one that gives relevance to the words, "I call heaven and earth to witness against you this day, that I have set before you life and death, blessing and curse; therefore choose life, ...'' (Deut. 30:19).

We judge by the choices we make and by the choices we make we are judged.

11. **Do you mean that there will be ''no Judgment Day''?**

I believe that the New Testament teaches that there will be a judgment day. What I have said is that there are two possibilities offered to us, life and death, and we determine which will be our destiny. John put the matter in these words ''For God so loved the world that he gave his only Son, that whosoever believes in him should not perish but have eternal life'' (John 3:16). So, by believing in Jesus as the Son of God we receive the gift of everlasting life.

Thus, when Christ who went up to heaven from a hill in Galilee (Acts 1:11) comes again to judge the living and the dead (II Tim. 4:1, I Pet. 4:5), we will be judged on the basis of the one ''law laid for us by God through Christ. This is the law of love.''[70]

God commanded that we love Him with the whole self and that we love our neighbor as we love self. He judges on the basis of that love.

I am of the conviction that Jesus himself provided for us an illustration of the Last Judgment. That illustration reveals its message both in words and in actions. In Matthew 25:31-46, in the future time of when the Son of man *comes* in his glory, the angels will *come* with him; he then *sits* on his glorious throne, all the nations of the earth are *gathered* before him, and he will *separate* the people into two groups and place one group; sheep, at his right hand, and goats at his left hand.

The sheep will inherit the kingdom prepared for them on the basis of their having actualized love of neighbor. By doing good unto "the least of these my brethren" the sheep "did it to me" was what they were told by the King.

The goats did not do good to the least of these, thus, they did not do good to the King, so by their own choices they selected for themselves their destiny "away into eternal punishment" (Matt. 25:46a).

12. **So, do we believe in "heaven and hell"?**

I get the impression from people's interest in hell that they want hell *for* other people. And I speak for myself when I say that I agree with Georgia Harkness when she wrote that, "Hell must not be thought of as physical torment or endless burning in a sea of fire. This is pictorial imagery like the pearly gates and streets of gold with which heaven is often pictured. The basic ideas in the meaning of hell are alienation and separation from God by persistent rejection of him, ..."[71]

So, Roger Shinn is on target with the preceding concept of hell as alienation from God with his definition. He wrote that, "To be offered love and to refuse it is hell. To disdain to trust the trustworthy is hell."[72]

On these two definitions and the words of Jesus spoken in the story of Lazarus and the rich man (St. Luke 16:19-31) I have my own description of hell. Of course, it must be understood as I believe that God made us for Himself and apart from a Father-child relationship with Him we have an unfulfilled yearning. A yearning and a longing that is unsettling yet while we are in the physical body the possibility exists that souls which thirst for God, for the living God, may indeed "come and behold the face of God" (Ps. 42:2).

Hell is to be created for love and to refuse the Divine love which actualizes human love (I John 4:10) and to die and be cut off from the hope of having the opportunity of believing in him who did in truth "rise from the dead" (Luke 16:31c).

Possibly, one of the hardest things to accept about "the torment" of hell is the truth that it is eternal. On the other hand, eternal is comforting for those who are heaven bound. Heaven is "the full consummation of the personal relationship to God which gives Christian life its meaning."[73] What begins in this life and grows into a loving relationship with God will be perfected as the reality expressed in the Revelation is unfolded. "Behold, the dwelling of God is with men. He will dwell with them, and they shall be his people, and God himself will be with them, he will wipe away every tear from their eyes, and death shall be no more, neither shall there be mourning nor crying nor pain any more, for the former things are passed away" (Rev. 21:3-4).

The relationship between God and His people as described above is not strained, the walls of hostility taken down by Jesus' death on the cross are not only still down, the relationship is transparent and the fellowship intimate. The environs are void of all tokens of the former life, all "former things are passed away," and this new world of which God said, "Behold, I make all things new" (Rev. 21:5b), it is indeed that of which God spoke to John, saying "It is done" (Rev. 21:6).

Chapter V

THE C.M.E. CHURCH

ORGANIZATION

1. **When was the C.M.E. Church organized?**

The organization of the C.M.E. Church took place on Friday, December 16, 1870. According to Bishop Othal H. Lakey[1] most of the delegates arrived on December 15, engaged in prayer and praise and did work in preparation for the official opening of the General Conference and the organization of the church.

2. **Where did the organization take place?**

The organization "conference convened in the 'spacious basement' of the First Methodist Episcopal Church, South, Jackson, Tennessee."[2]

3. **What were some of the things accomplished in the first General Conference?**

Some of the things done were (a) the adoption of the name "the Colored Methodist Episcopal Church in America"; (b) the adoption of the *Discipline* of the M.E. Church, South, making the changes necessary to suit it to the condition of the new church; (c) the continuation of *the Christian Index* as the official paper, and the election of Samuel Watson as editor; (d) the adoption of a resolution on December 19, the third day, looking forward to the creation of a Publishing House[3]; and (e) the election of two (2) bishops.

4. **What of the first name given to the new church?**

The original name, the Colored Methodist Episcopal Church in America, was significant for several reasons.[4] Colored was the name commonly used when referring to the former slaves. It was the term used to identify the race of the individuals who were members and organizers of the church. So they selected "Colored" to be part of the name of their church.

"Methodist" indicated the unbroken bond with the Methodist organization of John Wesley and with the organization of Methodism in America in 1784 in Baltimore, Maryland.

"Episcopal" was consonant with superintendency by bishops as the members of the C.M.E. Church in America had known of it in the M.E. Church, South. It was the form of church government known to them.

"Church" as institution of the people who belong to the Lord is what is expressed. And that institution and its people were "in America". The C.M.E. Church did not intend to be regarded as regional as was true of its parent body, the M.E. Church, South. It refused to limit how it would possibly be perceived with the adoption of a geographical term as part of its name. The use of Colored did not pose a problem since the expectation of whites becoming members was non-existent. But the adoption of the name C.M.E. Church, South, as had been proposed would have sent forth a message that they did not want.

5. **What happened to the original name, C.M.E. Church in America?**

Bishop Charles Henry Phillips wrote that "While there has been no great desire to change the name, there has been a desire to see the phrase, 'in America,' dropped; and this can, and doubtless will be done in the future, without any injury to the name of the Church."[5]

It appears that by 1930 the phrase "in America" did drop out of use.[6] That occurred without any official or unofficial action taking place. I suppose it happened in pretty much the same way as the dropping of a middle name happened for some persons. They just stopped using that part of their name.

Colored on the other hand was officially changed by the General Conference in 1954, with "Christian" being substituted for it.

It was determined that changing the name of the church was a "constitutional matter," thus, the General Conference action had to be ratified by two-thirds (2/3) majority of all members of the Annual Conferences.[7]

On January 19, 1956 in Detroit, Michigan the College of Bishops to which responsibility has been granted for announcing ratification results announced through its Secretary that the name change had received the votes necessary for ratification. So on January 19, 1956 the action of 1954 became effective.[8]

6. **Who were the two persons elected to the office of Bishop in 1870?**

The first bishop elected by the Colored Methodist Episcopal Church in America was William H. Miles. He was born in Springfield, Washington County, Kentucky, December 26, 1828. He was forty-one (41) years old. So close to forty-two, but, not quite there.

The second preacher elected bishop in this church was Richard H. Vanderhorst, who was born December 15, 1813, in Georgetown, South Carolina. It is very likely that Vanderhorst celebrated his 57th birthday in Jackson, Tennessee on the eve of the official opening of the First General Conference of what would become the C.M.E. Church in America.

STRUCTURE

1. **How would you describe the structure of the C.M.E. Church?**

   Basically our government consists of three branches. Which are the Legislative; the Executive and the Judicial.

2. **Will you expand on the three branches of our government?**

   Provided the analogy is not carried too far, the three branches may be compared to the federal government of the United States of America.

   First of all let me point out that each of the three is constitutional. That is, each is authorized and undergirded by specific provisions in the Constitution of the C.M.E. Church.[9]

   The Legislative Branch is the General Conference. In the Federal government the Congress is the legislative branch. We carried this one over from the Methodist Episcopal Church when we organized in 1870. In fact the College of Bishops of the C.M.E. Church ruled when it was also the Judicial Branch that the First General Conference was indeed such by virtue of it having been duly authorized and called and because it performed the duties incumbent upon that body as had been done historically in American Methodism and as the General Conference in our church had continued to do subsequent to 1870.

   The President of the United States along with his advisors and cabinet constitute the Executive Branch in our Federal government. In this church the College of Bishops is the Executive Branch. The College exists with the mandate to ''meet at least once a year and plan for the general oversight and promotion of the temporal and spiritual interests of the entire church and for carrying into effect the rules, regulations, and responsibilities prescribed and enjoined by the General Conference.''[10]

Also, the Articles of Incorporation state, thus, ''The spiritual leaders of this Church, religious and temporal, shall be the College of Bishops.''[11]

The Judicial Branch of this church is the Judicial Council of which the U.S. Supreme Court is its counterpart. It is the youngest of the branches. Prior to 1950 judicial authority resided in the College of Bishops.[12] The transfer of judicial authority took place in 1950, but it must be pointed out that the efforts to effect a separate branch and the efforts to bring about the transfer after the authorization for a separate branch was voted by the General Conference have histories embracing more than a generation.[13]

THE STRUCTURE INTERPRETED

General Conference

1. **What is the background of the General Conference in American Methodism?**

I stated earlier that this body as part of the polity of the M.E. Church, South has always been part of our polity. However, it has not always been part of Methodism. The history of the representative General Conference began in 1808. Prior to that time it seems as though all preachers could attend what may have been the yearly meeting or ''a general convention''. Francis Asbury called the first such conference to meet at Baltimore, Maryland Christmas week 1784, and basic to the call was Asbury's insistence that the preachers vote their consent for him to exercise the ordination as superintendent that John Wesley had bestowed. And some historians maintain that "these men," that is, those who "elected" Asbury in 1784, "represented the connection completely as they met at this memorable gathering."[14]

So while the first "Conference" was held by John Wesley in 1744 with those preachers with whom he desired to confer and met annually thereafter,[15] the representative General Conference was voted into existence in 1808 by the Methodist preachers who gave their authority over to that body. And despite the schism of 1844 which divided the Methodist Episcopal Church into North and South the General Conference continued and became part of our organization in 1870.

2. **Who constitutes General Conference?**

The Annual Conferences elect delegates, the same number of each, clergy and lay representatives, according to their memberships. At this time each Annual Conference may elect one delegate, that is, one clergy and one lay representative for every twenty-one (21) members of the Annual Conference. Which means that the number of members is calculated by adding the number of Preachers in Full Connection and the number of delegates elected by the local charges to the Annual Conference.

The number delegates that a conference is eligible to elect may be found by dividing the number of members by twenty one. For a major fraction over one additional delegate, one lay and one clergy, may be elected.[16]

The Bishops are ex-officio members of General Conference. They have *voice to speak* but they do not have "the privilege of debate or vote."[17]

3. **When does the General Conference meet?**

I maintain that the General Conference is basically an abstraction and as such it exists only when it meets. It has no continuing membership. The Annual Conference by contrast has in its preachers "ipso facto" members[18] who give it continuity.

So the General Conference meets in quadrennial session or every four years "for nine days between June 15 and July 15 commencing on a Saturday."[19]

Provisions exist for call sessions.[20]

4. **What constitutionally granted powers have been delegated to the General Conference?**

The General Conference shall have full powers to make rules and regulations for the Church subject to the limitations of the restrictive rules and in the exercise of this power shall have authorities as follows:

a. To define and fix the conditions, privileges and duties of Church membership.
b. To define and fix the powers and duties of elders, deacons, probationers, supply preachers, local preachers and exhorters.
c. To define and fix the powers and duties of Annual Conferences, District Conferences, Quarterly Conferences, Church Conferences and Official Boards.
d. To provide for the organization, promotion and administration of the work of the Church outside of the United States of America.

e. To determine and provide for raising the funds necessary to carry on the Connectional work of the church.
f. To define and fix the powers and duties of the Pastors in Charge and the Presiding Elders.
g. To define and fix the powers, duties, and privileges of the Episcopacy; to adopt a plan for the support of the Bishops; to provide for the discontinuance of a Bishop because of incfficiency or unacceptability.
h. To regulate all matters relating to the form and mode of worship, ritual, and religious services and ceremonies subject to the limitations of the First Restrictive rule.
i. To provide a judicial system and a method of judicial procedure for the Church.
j. To initiate and to direct all Connectional enterprises of the Church (such as publishing, evangelistic, missionary and benevolent) and to provide boards for their promotion and administration.
k. To enact such other legislation as may be necessary, subject to the limitations and restrictions of the Constitution of the Church.[21]

Annual Conference

1. **What is the Annual Conference?**

An Annual Conference is a continuous, basic unit of the Christian Methodist Episcopal Church existing as a geographic entity and constituted by the several pastoral charges within the geographic area. It is a yearly meeting consisting of the ministerial members, active and retired, who are in full connection therein, the probationary members, or members on trial, and the duly elected lay delegates by the local charges to its session, with all rights, duties, obligations, and/or responsibilities of its members, pursuant to the *Discipline* of the Christian Methodist Episcopal Church.[22]

2. **How are the members of the Annual Conference selected?**

Let us begin with the preachers who are in full connection with an Annual Conference. Their membership is granted by vote of those preachers who are already members. The process leading to the vote starts with the laity voting in the Quarterly Conference to recommend one of its members, a local preacher, for admission on trial in the traveling connection with that Annual Conference. A committee in the Annual Conference exists to work with the recommendations and it brings the persons to the floor with its own recommendation. After staying on trial for two or more years, meeting all requirements during that period, the preacher promises to do certain things. After vowing, the preacher is voted into the Conference as a voting member.[23]

Lay members of the Annual Conference in session are elected to it by the Church Conference. This is done each year. Also, the representatives of each local charge must be certified by the Quarterly Conference.

3. **What are some of the key functions of the Annual Conference?**

Some of the key functions are authorizing Bishops to ordain the persons it selects to be Deacons and Elders in the Church; administering discipline with love; electing representatives to General Conference, and voting on constitutional matters presented to it.

District Conference

1. **What is a District Conference?**

The answer to what is a District Conference requires first an answer to the question: What is a District? In the C.M.E. Church we have the Episcopal District which refers to the group of Annual Conferences over which a bishop is assigned. We use "District" also in referring to a number of churches or charges within an Annual Conference and over which the Bishop appoints a preacher under the heading "Presiding Elder". When the pastors, local preachers, and lay delegates who have been elected by their Quarterly Conference meet together on the call of the Presiding Elder that body in assembly is the District Conference.

2. **How often does it meet?**

Since this is a permissive conference, it is proper to say it "may be held annually."

The time of its meeting shall be set by the Presiding Elder.

3. **Who is the Presiding Officer?**

The Presiding Elder over the district shall preside in the session of the District Conference. But if the Presiding Elder is absent the Conference shall elect a President.

4. **What does the Presiding Elder's District in Conference meet to do?**

It examines Journals of the Quarterly Conference. It inquires into the condition of the several charges of the District. It holds discussions and gives prominence to preaching, prayer, love feast and Holy Communion. It is to be an occasion for spiritual as well as theological enrichment.

The Quarterly Conference

1. **What is the Quarterly Conference?**

The Quarterly Conference is a mandated body in the C.M.E. Church and it is also the traditional business and governing body of the Local Charge.[24] It is important to the health and well-being of the local church because if the church's business is rightly transacted in Quarterly Conference proper procedures will be followed, and proper authority granted for the execution of business. Also, from this body the connection receives through the Presiding Elder statistics, and reports and information on the local church regarding its spiritual health and welfare.

2. **Who are its members?**

The membership includes the Pastor, the officers of the local church, choirsters who are members of that charge, exhorters, and local preachers.

3. **How often does it meet?**

The name Quarterly Conference suggests four meetings a year. However, the *Discipline* states that it "may meet four times a year". And it provides also for "special or call sessions."[25]

4. **Who presides?**

The Presiding Elder presides without the privilege of vote. In his or her absence the Preacher in Charge shall preside.

5. **What are some of its functions?**

Some of its duties are to elect persons to key positions as officers and leaders. However, the basic core group of officers consisting of Stewards, Stewardesses, and Trustees as well as several others are first *selected* by and recommended by the Pastor before being *elected* by the Quarterly Conference.

It also licenses persons to exhort and to preach; it recommends preachers to the Annual Conference for admission on trial and for local deacon and elder's orders; it certifies delegates elected by the Church Conference to Annual Conference, and it elects delegates to the District Conference.

It votes on all matters pertaining to real estate such as buying and selling land and buildings, and it votes on approval for building of facilities for church or for a parsonage and etc., and it votes on borrowing money to buy, build, or remodel properties. An affirmative vote is necessary for approval. And after that has been done the Presiding Elder and the Bishop must give written consent for transactions to proceed lawfully.

The Church Conference

1. **What is the Church Conference?**

It is a body supported by constitutional mandate[26] and consisting of all the members and resident members of the Annual Conference at every pastoral appointment.

2. **What is the historical background of the Church Conference?**

"In the technical meaning" of Church Conference, it was "an organization peculiar to the polity of the Methodist Episcopal Church, South, at the time of union."[28]

As I noted earlier in passing the big split in the M.E. Church took place in 1844. Before then, in 1828, the Methodist Protestant group as it was named split off. In 1939 the Union of the M.E. Church, and the Methodist Protestant Church and the M.E. Church, South took place and the METHODIST Church was organized. It merged with the Evangelical United Brethren Church in 1968 and the United Methodist Church came to be.

Back to the discussion on the Church Conference and the note that this body originated in the M.E. Church, South in 1866.[29]

So, as part of the polity of the M.E. Church, South it came as part of the *Discipline* that we adopted in 1870.

3. **How often does it meet?**

It shall meet once a month in station charges and at least once every three months in circuits. And it should meet when the bulk of the members can meet. Except, it should not be scheduled so as to interfere with Sunday worship services.

4. **Who presides in the Church Conference?**

"The Preacher in Charge shall preside."[30] And there is no disciplinary provision providing for anyone else to call or to hold a Church Conference.

5. **What are some of its duties?**

It provides the setting for examining the roll of members of the church. It hears reports from the

Pastor and from the church organizations. It looks into the conditions of the poor among its own. It considers whether the charge is or is not doing its part for missions. It looks at whether or not the askings of the Annual Conference are being collected. It asks if its members are buying, circulating and reading C.M.E. produced or distributed literature. It asks about ways to extend its work as a church and how it may strengthen its community witness.

The Church Conference elects delegates to the Annual Conference. This may be done at any meeting and it should not be left until the end of the Annual Conference year is at hand since the Quarterly Conference must certify the delegates elected.[31]

The Official Board

1. **What is the Official Board?**

   It is "The Official or Leaders' Meeting."[32]

2. **What is its historical background?**

   Bishop Nolan B. Harmon noted that in the M.E. Church, North, the Official Board developed as churches grew larger in memberships and with urbanization stewards and trustees who made up the bulk of the Quarterly Conference recognized the need for monthly rather than quarterly meetings in which to conduct business. So on an unofficial basis they held official board meetings and with its rise brought to the attention of the Methodist Episcopal Church it authorized the Quarterly Conference to organize and continue at its pleasure an Official Board. That authorization appeared in the 1908 *Discipline* of the M.E. Church. But the M.E. Church, South, though it had Official Boards composed almost entirely of stewards, never gave formal recognition in its *Discipline* to them.[33]

3. **What is the Official Board's relationship to the Church Conference or to the Quarterly Conference?**

I regard the Official Board as the executive and administrative arm of the Quarterly Conference. By which I mean that it exists in part to supervise and to monitor the carrying out of the decisions of the Quarterly Conference in specific matters such as those related to real estate and to carry on the general business of the local congregation.

Its relationship to the Church Conference could be termed supervisory in that actions taken by Church Conference and the responsibility delegated to an organization or board for executing them would fall to the Official Board in which officers meet.

Some persons in our church consider the Official Board solely the administrative arm of the Church Conference.

4. **When does it meet and what does it meet to do?**

It is to meet weekly. And as the title suggests it is a meeting of church officers with the Pastor presiding. And it is to consider what I call nurturing and disciplinary concerns; and pastoral and financial interests.

Judicial Administration and the Judicial Council

1. **Is our Judicial System limited to Judicial Council?**

No. It is not. Judicial authority and responsibility have been given by the church to some conferences, committees and individuals. For example, in trial and appeal matters pertaining to bishops the General Conference is the court of last resort. For ministerial members of the Annual Conference that body has final say in trial matters on appeal. Lay members are tried by a Court of Peers from their local church and appeals for lay members are handled by a committee from the District appointed by the Presiding Elder.

For detailed specifics you should consult the *Discipline*. My intention here is to deal with the fact that judicial duties are handled by several bodies and to lift up the principle of judgment by peers.

An additional aspect of the question, thus, of the answer is that interpreting our laws and rendering decisions and receiving and hearing written complaints and appeals are part of the duties of Presiding Elders *in the Quarterly Conference* and Bishops when presiding *in the* Annual Conference. So those judicial functions are given to certain offices and by inference based on hearing appeals in Quarterly Conference pastors interpret laws in Church Conference or Official Board meetings.

2. **Do you mean that every member of the C.M.E. Church is subject to discipline?**

Yes. Every member, clerical and lay, is subject to trial. But more significant is the fact that the Fifth Restrictive Rule protects "the privilege of our Ministers or Preachers of trial by a committee and of an appeal." And, it says also that the General Conference shall not "do away with the privileges of our members of trial before the Church or by a committee, and of an appeal."

3. **Is the Judicial Council a trial court?**

The Judicial Council is an appellate body. The appeals it hears are those on decisions Bishops' write on questions of law coming before them in Annual Conference; those on appeals regarding the constitutionality of acts of General Conference; and those appeals on the legality of acts of the Annual Conference or the General Connectional Board.[35]

No. It is not a trial court. It tries no one.

4. **What is the Judicial Council?**

It is the council of last resort in that its decisions are final on matters coming before it on appeal and in the declaratory decisions it renders.

It is an appellate body but it has the power to render declaratory decisions. If the General Conference had disallowed direct access to the Council for declaratory decisions it would be purely appellate. In that before a member could petition the Council for an interpretation of a law the member would have to exhaust the appeal process. After doing so, appeal would be made to the Council for a declaratory decision.

At present any member may petition the Council. However, our law does say on this matter: "It is an abuse of the declaratory privilege to by-pass the appellate procedure."[36]

5. **How many members are there on the Judicial Council and how do they get on it?**

The Council is composed of nine active members, five lay and four clergy, elected by General Conference. The College of Bishops nominates twice the number of lay persons and twice the number of clergy persons to be elected in each session of General Conference. Nominations may be made from the floor.

The delegates to General Conference vote their election to the Council.

Starting with the General Conference in 1986 a schedule was set up with staggered terms so as to avoid the likelihood of having to elect an entirely new Council at one time.

Also, the General Conference elects alternates and they serve in the event of a vacancy. They serve according to their order of election, first, second, etc. And ministers fill vacancies in the ministerial ranks and lay alternates fill vacancies in the lay ranks.

Like others serving at the general level by election all members of the Council retire at the General Conference nearest their 74th birthday.

6. **Are the members paid salary?**

The members of the Council do not receive salary. An annual allocation is provided in the Connectional Budget for the expenses of the Council.

7. **Since the College of Bishops nominates and the General Conference elects the Council members is it "equal" with the other two branches of our government?**

Regarding the nominating responsibility of the College of Bishops it is tempered of any privilege on the College's part, first, by the right of members to make nominations from the floor; second, by the right of General Conference to elect; and third, by the fact that the responsibility to nominate is a grant from General Conference and not a right inherent in the College of Bishops.

So the role of the College of Bishops, basically, is to insure an orderly process.

Regarding the role of the General Conference, it is always important to remember not *what*, but *who* that body is. The General Conference *is the people.* It is the C.M.E. Church in assembly and the power in this church is with the people. The College of Bishops and the Judicial Council are because the people as the General Conference said, "Let there be" and both bodies are.

Equality and independence are not in who participate in the process of election. Rather, they are in the authority granted the Judicial Council by the people of the C.M.E. Church speaking in General Conference.

8. **So, how long have we had a Judicial Council?**

For many years the College of Bishops acted in the capacity of the judiciary. That procedure was pretty much if not completely the way of all so-called major Methodist denominations. The practice exists yet. But in 1930 the General Conference of our church acted to authorize a "Judicial Committee" but it was not established. In 1950 the Judicial Council became operative on a law passed by General Conference in 1946.[37]

Episcopal, Episcopacy and Bishops

1. **What do we mean by an "Episcopal form of government"?**

It means that a church is governed or superintended by bishops. However, in the C.M.E. Church that does not mean that bishops "run the Church". For bishops cannot do as they please. They are persons under law in a church of law.

What it does mean is that by its Constitution and its Articles of Incorporation the people have by the former given them as a group "general oversight" and in the latter designated them "The spiritual leaders of this Church, religious and temporal" as "the College of Bishops."

2. **What is "episcopacy"?**

It is used in the collective sense when referring to bishops. "The Episcopacy" is also an abstraction and may refer to the office of bishop. So usually we mean one or the other, the College as the Bishops as a group or as a collegial body, or in the second place, we mean an office to which one aspires or to which a person has been elected.

3. **What do we mean by bishops?**

Bishops are ordained elders in the Church of God who were elected by the majority vote of General Conference and were consecrated to the office by the laying on of hands by other bishops and elders.

Bishops are symbols of the unity, authority, and continuity of the Church. As representative and general ministers bishops in collegiality represent the whole of the C.M.E. Church; in the administration of discipline bishops exercise authority; and through the laying on of hands in ordination they pass on the continuity of the Church of which they are token.

Bishops are pastors, priests, and prophets called of Christ to share his ministry. They are preachers of the Gospel, administrators of the Holy Sacraments, teachers, shepherds in whose charge and care the whole church is committed as the College of Bishops and portions committed to each bishop as Presiding Bishops of Episcopal Districts.

Bishops are representatives of the C.M.E. Church in and to ecumenical bodies, such as, the World Methodist Council, the World Council of Churches, the National Council of Churches, the Consultation On Church Union, and the Congress Of National Black Churches.

4. **What is the College of Bishops?**
The College of Bishops is the forum in which the Bishops active and retired must meet at least once a year to act for the spiritual welfare of the whole church.

General Church Agencies

1. **How do General Boards and Departments fit into our government?**
If we were exactly like the Federal Government these agencies would be "the cabinet" of the College of Bishops in pretty much the same way as the Secretaries are members of the cabinet of the President. But that is not the case. The departments have by-laws by which they are governed and they function according to their by-laws either as "Connectional Program Ministries" or as "Connectional Operation." The heads of these agencies are elected by General Conference and a Bishop serves as Chair of the body that supervises their work. The College of Bishops elects the Chair for each "Committee" as most are called.
General agencies are ministries in the operations of the C.M.E. Church as it engages in mission. They are not essentially governmental; they are operatives created and continued for inner directed and outer directed services.

2. **What holds them together?**
The General Connectional Board supervises "the administration of the connectional program."

3. **What is the General Connectional Board?**

It is a body established by General Conference and is composed of representatives from the several Episcopal Districts of the church.

The members of each District are elected by its delegates to the General Conference and are presented to and certified by the General Conference.

It meets annually except when General Conference meets and all General Officers report to it. The Senior Bishop is the Chairperson.

4. **What are the names of the General Agencies?**

The agencies are divided into two divisions. One is called ''Connectional Ministries.'' It is comprised of the Departments of Christian Education; Lay Ministry; and Evangelism, Missions, and Human Concerns.

The other division is ''Connectional Operations'' and it is made up of the Departments of Finance; Publications; and Personnel Services.

5. **Who heads each?**

Each agency is headed by a General Secretary elected by General Conference. Each of them is immediately under the supervision of a ''Standing Committee'' whose members are assigned by a special committee. One of the Bishops is assigned to serve as Chair of each Standing Committee by the College of Bishops.

6. **What are the titles of the General Officers?**

The General Officers of the Christian Methodist Episcopal Church shall be:

The Executive Secretary of the C.M.E. Church

The Editor of *The Christian Index*

The General Secretary of Christian Education
The General Secretary of Lay Ministry
The General Secretary of Evangelism, Missions, and Human Concerns
The General Secretary of Finance
The General Secretary of Publications
The General Secretary of Personnel Services
The President of The Women's Connectional Council

7. **Again, who is responsible for the program of the General Church?**

The program agencies along with the General Connectional Board share collective responsibility for getting it together and for getting it out. The Bishops have responsibility to promote it.

WOMEN'S MISSIONARY COUNCIL

1. **When was the Women's Missionary Council organized?**

It was first organized in September of 1918 at Capers Chapel C.M.E. Church, Nashville, Tennessee.

2. **Who was its first President?**

Dr. Mattie E. Coleman was elected the first President. Others elected since Dr. Coleman are: Mrs. Rossie T. Hollis 1939-1955; Mrs. E.W.F. Harris, 1955-1963; Mrs. Phyllis H. Bedford 1963-1971; Mrs. Pauline B. Grant 1971 1979; Mrs. Thelma J. Dudley 1979-1987; Dr. Sylvia M. Faulk 1987-.

3. **What is its chief executive officer called?**

The chief executive officer is called "President."

4. **Is the President paid the same salary as other General Officers?**

   The salary of the President is the same as the other salaried General Officers.

5. **Where is the authority of the W.M.C.?**

   It is in the Assembly that is held quadrennially. An Executive Board meets in the other years.

6. **How does the Women's Missionary Council function?**

   This discussion is limited to the levels of the W.M.C.'s operations which parallel the structure of our church. Thus, the Council's work is done through its three divisions, which are: (a) Structure; (b) Program; and (c) Service and Outreach, which are headed by Secretaries. In addition the Council Standing Committees, are Finance, Nominating, and Constitution and By-Laws; and with the President, the Assembly also elects a Vice President, Secretary Assistant Secretary, Treasurer, and Editor of *the Missionary Messenger*, the official publications of the Council; all share in its functioning.

   From the Council each conference level, Annual, District, and Local has a Women's Missionary Society.

Chapter VI

THE ORDAINED MINISTRY AND THE LOCAL CHURCH

THE LOCAL MINISTRY

1. **What is a Local Preacher?**

The best way to understand the Local Preacher is to know that there is also a class of Preacher known as Traveling Preachers.

A Local Preacher is a person who has been examined by the Quarterly Conference, passed, and the Quarterly Conference authorized a license to be issued by the Presiding Elder, who along with the Secretary of the Quarterly Conference sign it, and the license issued.

The key word is *Local* in understanding the difference between a Local and a Traveling Preacher. Local means the Preacher may use the license in the Charqe to which he or she belongs and which authorized it. A Traveling Preacher is one who travels or moves about under the authority of an Annual Conference and the Presiding Bishop.

A Local Preacher is under his or her local church pastor and is amenable for his or her conduct to the Quarterly Conference. The Local Preacher's License must be renewed yearly.

2. **What is a Local Deacon?**

A Local Deacon is a Local Preacher who has been ordained in an annual conference by a Bishop at the request of the Quarterly Conference of the charge to which the Local Preacher belongs. Again, *Local* is the key word. A Local Deacon may use the order only in the local charge which requested ordination.

A Local Deacon is not a Traveling Preacher, even though he or she may perform the same functions as a Traveling Deacon. The difference is *WHERE* they can be performed.

3. **What is a Local Elder?**

The Local Elder can perform the same functions as a Traveling Elder. The same difference applies here as is true of the Local Deacon. It is *WHERE* a Local Elder can lawfully use the order. Again, as minister of Word and Sacrament the order may be used only in the charge that asked that the Local Deacon be ordained Local Elder, except when permission is given by a superior.

4. **What is a Local Pastor?**

A minister not in full connection, but pastors a church.

TRAVELING PREACHERS

1. **How many ministerial orders are there?**

There are two (2) orders.

2. **What are the names of the orders?**

The two orders are: Deacon and Elder.

3. **What is a deacon?**

A Deacon is an Elder's helper or assistant and cannot function as a priest in baptism and in performing the wedding ceremony except in the absence of an Elder. A deacon may not consecrate the elements used in the sacrament of Holy Communion.

4. **How is a preacher made a deacon?**

A Traveling Deacon comes from among the ranks of Preachers on trial in an annual conference. In order to be made a Deacon, the Preacher must pass an approved examination upon the Bishops Course of Study; must have traveled for one year; must be elected to the order by the Annual Conference which votes only after a favorable recommendation has been made by the Committee On Examination. The Bishop lays on hands in the ordination.

5. **What is an elder?**

A Traveling Elder is a full-fledged minister of Word and Sacrament.

6. **How is a preacher made an elder?**

A Traveling Deacon is *eligible* after meeting other requirements which are: must pass an approved examination upon the Bishops Course of Study; must be recommended by the Committee on Ministerial Examination; must receive the majority vote of the members of the Annual Conference.

The Bishop assisted by some of the Traveling Elders lay on hands.

7. **What are the duties of an elder?**

The Traveling Elder has authority to: administer the Sacraments; to perform the rite of holy matrimony, to bury the dead, to conduct all parts of Divine worship; and to do all of the duties of a Traveling Preacher.

8. **What is "full connection"?**

Full connection is the status given by vote of the Annual Conference to a Preacher on trial in the conference. It means that a preacher is a full-fledged member of an Annual Conference with all rights, privileges and responsibilities. It means that the Preacher is no longer a member of a local church.

9. **What is "a superannuated preacher"?**

A Superannuated Preacher is a Retired Preacher.

10. **What is "a supernumerated preacher"?**

A Supernumerated Preacher is a preacher who is on leave from traveling due to health or other extenuating circumstances.

11. **What is "a located preacher"?**

A Located Preacher is a preacher whose membership with an Annual Conference has been dissolved by the Annual Conference and returned to a Quarterly Conference. Location may be granted upon request of the Preacher or it may be imposed by initiative of the Conference.

12. **When should a preacher be called "Reverend"?**

Calling a preacher Reverend should be reserved for the order of Deacon. The law of the Church prohibits wearing clerical collars until the order of deacon has been bestowed.

13. **What are the three offices of the ordered ministry?**

The three are Pastor; Presiding Elder; and Bishop.

14. **How is a preacher made a bishop?**

A Bishop is constituted by the vote of the General Conference and by consecration through the laying on of hands of three Bishops or at least one Bishop and two elders.

If there are no Bishops left to serve, the General Conference shall elect a Bishop, and three Elders chosen by the General Conference shall consecrate the Bishop-elect.

15. **What is a presiding elder?**

A Presiding Elder is a Traveling Elder who presides over a District within an Annual Conference.

16. **How is a presiding elder made?**

The Bishop presiding in an Annual Conference appoints an Elder to serve as a Presiding Elder.

17. **How is a local charge pastor made?**

By the appointment to a local charge by a Bishop in an annual conference.

THE LOCAL CHURCH

Definitions

1. **What is a Local Charge?**

A Local Charge is an appointment over which a pastor in charge is assigned by a Bishop in an Annual Conference.

2. **Is a church and a charge one and the same?**

A pastoral charge may be either a station, consisting of one church, or it may be an enlarged charge, consisting of several autonomous churches placed under the same pastor but shall maintain separate officers. It shall be known as an enlarged charge with each church having the right to elect its delegates to the District and Annual Conferences.

3. **What is a mission?**

A mission is a charge with less than fifty (50) members.

Administrator

1. **Who is the Chief Administrator of the Local Church?**

The Preacher in Charge is the Chief Administrator of the Local Church.[1]

2. **What does it mean to say that the Pastor is Chief Administrator?**

It does not mean that the Pastor is boss or dictator. It does not mean that the Pastor's way is the way, and that he or she runs the whole show.

It means that the Pastor administers. The things that the Pastor ministers are planned, authorized and approved in Church Conference or Official Board.

The Pastor does not carry all of the things into action that have been approved. Giving oversight to the whole program is different from doing everything. The Chief Administrator concept intends to establish the symbol of unity and to put in clear terms that responsibility for overseeing the execution of the program is put in one office, that of Pastor.

The Chief Administrator is part of the planning for the program of a local church since someone has to start the ball rolling, so to speak. The role continues through the assignment of various tasks and goes on to giving oversight to the execution of the plans. It is both a people ministry and a program functionaire.

OFFICERS AND ORGANIZATIONS

Stewards

1. **What is a steward?**

A steward is a church member who has been selected for the office of steward by the Pastor and elected by the Quarterly Conference upon the Pastor's recommendation.

2. **What are some of the duties of stewards?**

Stewards in a general way are responsible for the finances of the local church. They do not own nor control the money. They are to see that the church has money to care for its obligations.

They associate the Stewardesses in estimating the annual salary and expenses of the Pastor.

They have spiritual and shepherding oversight of members and are to care for them, along with the sick and the disorderly.

Traditionally, stewards have been regarded as part of the Pastor's cabinet.

Stewards provide housing for the Pastor where the church does not have a parsonage. And they provide the elements for the sacrament of Holy Communion.

3. **How long is a steward elected to serve?**

A steward serves one year at a time and must be selected by the Pastor and elected by the Quarterly Conference, annually. So, once a steward is not always a steward.

4. **What qualifications are there for being a steward?**

A steward must be a person of solid piety, must know and love Methodist doctrine and discipline, and must have natural or acquired ability to transact the temporal affairs of a church.

5. **Can a steward act on his or her own in the name of a church?**

No. Stewards are organized into the Steward Board with a Chairman, Secretary, and Treasurer.

Further, no member of a church may obligate it financially without the consent of the Official Board, or Church Conference or Quarterly Conference.

6. **To whom are stewards accountable?**

They are accountable to the Quarterly Conference.

7. **What is a Recording Steward?**

A Recording Steward is a steward whom the Quarterly Conference elected upon the recommendation of the Pastor.

8. **What does a Recording Steward do?**

The Recording Steward is a key person for good church administration. He or she is custodian of the records of the Quarterly Conference, where there is no church office.

The record of the financial income and expenditures of the church, that means all monies raised in the name of the church should be kept by the Recording Steward. And a report of the same made to the Quarterly Conference and to the Annual Conference. Also, that information shall be given to the Pastor whenever requested.

In order for a Recording Steward to work efficiently, there must be reports made by all who raise money. The reports may be made in the Official Board or the Church Conference. And the money turned over to a treasurer for the church who receipts the Board of Stewards and deposited in a bank chosen by a local church body, the Official Board or the Church Conference.

9. **How does a church determine how many stewards to elect?**

By its membership. It may elect one for every thirty (30) members. On a circuit each church may have at least one steward and each circuit or station may have at least seven.

Stewardesses

1. **How are stewardesses elected?**

They are nominated to the Quarterly Conference by the Pastor and elected by that body.

2. **If the Quarterly Conference refuses to elect the nominees of the Pastor, what then?**

The Quarterly Conference may only vote up or down the nominees of the Pastor. It does not have authority to question the selection nor to make selections. This holds true in all cases where the Pastor makes the selections.

3. **What are some of the duties of Stewardesses?**

They serve the table of the Lord, the table of the poor, and the table of the ministry.

So, then, stewardesses take care of the linen and the cups and glasses used for Holy Communion. They provide for the needy. And they participate with the Board of Stewards in estimating the salary and traveling expenses of the Pastor.

Stewardesses assist in baptism by preparing for it and by placing linen on the candidates.

Stewardesses *are not* authorized to serve the sacrament of Holy Communion. The preparation of un-consecrated elements is a far different matter than serving the consecrated elements.

Trustees

1. **How are trustees made?**

The Pastor selects individuals and nominates them to the Quarterly Conference which elects trustees.

In the absence of a pastor, the Presiding Elder may nominate and the Quarterly Conference elects.

The importance of the office may be seen in the fact that in the absence of a pastor provision is made for the election of trustees.

2. **How many trustees may a church elect?**

It may elect three, five, seven, or nine. They must be members of the C.M.E. Church.

3. **Is there a minimum age for election as a trustee?**

Yes. A local church trustee must be eighteen years of age at the time of election.

4. **What are some of their duties?**

Trustees of an incorporated church make up the Board of Directors of the Corporation.

Trustees are custodians of church property, real, personal, and mixed. They see that insurance coverage is carried on the church and all church properties.

Trustees report to the Quarterly Conference which has authority over them, and to which they are amenable for their conduct and performance of their duties.

5. **Can trustees obligate the church financially?**

They may obligate the church only with the permission of the Official Board, or the Church Conference or the Quarterly Conference.

6. **What provision is made for dealing with trustees who disobey the orders of the Official Board, or the Church Conference, or the Quarterly Conference?**

Automatic dismissal is the provision provided for one, or several, or the entire Board of Trustees who disobey the orders of one of the above stated bodies.

The exception to the dismissal is where state or territorial statutes provide to the contrary.

Treasurer

1. **How is the Treasurer elected?**
The Pastor nominates a church member to the Quarterly Conference, it elects.

2. **What are the duties?**
Those commonly performed in the office, except in our church, the Recording Steward makes reports that treasurers in some other organizations make.

Class Leaders

1. **How are Class Leaders appointed?**
They are appointed by the Pastor in Charge.

2. **What requirements are there for selecting members to be Class Leaders?**
Their moral and spiritual life should reflect persons of sound judgment and true devotion to God.
They should be examined by the Pastor at least once monthly on their methods of leading the classes.

3. **What do Class Leaders do?**
Class Leaders visit their members once a week, for at least three reasons. One, to see how their souls prosper. Two, to comfort, advise, or reprove them. Three, to receive what they are willing to give towards the support of the Pastor and the poor.
They meet weekly with the Pastor and the Stewards to report what has happened and collected in their visitations.

Christian Education

1. **Under which organization is the program of Christian Education housed?**
   The Board of Christian Education is the parent body of the program of Christian Education.

2. **How is the Board organized?**
   The Board is constituted by action of the Quarterly Conference. The Pastor is ex-officio Chairperson and has responsibility for nominating members for the Board who, in some instances, are the elected representatives of organizations of the Local Church. The Quarterly Conference elects the members.
   After the election the Pastor should call the members together and organize the Board.

3. **How is the policy and program of Christian Education made and who carries them out?**
   The Board makes policy and develops program. The Director of Christian Education executes policy and program. General supervision of educational work in the Local Church is under the Director.

4. **How is the Director of Christian Education elected.**
   The Pastor appoints a person as Director and the Quarterly Conference confirms the appointee.

Sunday School

1. **How does the Sunday School fit into this program?**
   The Sunday School is one of several units that make up the Christian Education ministry. It is not an independent group.

The Sunday School is under the administrative guidance of a General Superintendent, who is under the Director of Christian Education.[2]

2. **How is the General Superintendent constituted?**
 The Pastor selects a person and presents the person to the Board of Christian Education for election. After the election, the Superintendent is presented to the Quarterly Conference for confirmation.

3. **How are Sunday School teachers chosen?**
 The officers and teachers are elected, in cooperation with the Pastor, by the Local Board of Christian Education.[3]

4. **How is the choice made on what Sunday School literature shall be used?**
 It is the duty of the Board of Christian Education to see that literature approved by the General Board of Christian Education is used in all teaching in our local churches.
 The Pastor as Minister of the Word has the responsibility for maintaining ''right teaching'' in the Local Church. Thus, the literature used in a C.M.E. Church is the concern of the Pastor since all printed materials used for religious instruction contains a point of view, a theology, and a certain slant in its understanding, interpretation, and presentation of Holy Scripture. It is never neutral.

Youth and Young Adults

1. **What are the names of the Youth and Young Adult organizations?**
 The names are the Christian Youth Fellowship and the Young Adult Council.

2. **Are these independent groups?**
   No. They are part of the Board of Christian Education.

3. **Who is the leader of each?**
   The President is the administrative officer of each.

Evangelism

1. **What is the name of the organization over evangelism in the local church?**
   The name of the group is the Commission on Membership and Evangelism.

2. **How is the Commission on Membership and Evangelism constituted?**
   There are no directions in the *Discipline* on organizing the Commission. Except it is to be made up of representatives of "the various organizations of the church".[4] It may be assumed that in view of the preceding that each organization selects its representative after the Pastor has provided leadership in the matter. And once the reprentatives are chosen the Pastor calls them together for organizing the Commission.

3. **Now that at the General Church evangelism is grouped with Mission and Human Concerns how has that affected the local church structure?**
   The re-structure of the General Department did not effect new organizations in the local church. Which does not mean that a local church may not combine the three functions. In many churches the memberships are too small to have three separate groups. And in churches with larger memberships the lack of interest, time, or talent may prohibit three groups

or the enhancement of efficiency and ministry may be positively served by a single organization in which three ministries are combined.

4. **Where does the local program of evangelism come from?**

The *Discipline* states that the local commission "shall work in cooperation with the Pastor, Presiding Elder and the District Director of Evangelism." What is being pointed to is a program coming to the local church from the General Department of Evangelism. However, it is probably true that the program that serves a local church best is one that is basically local in design and is enabled by the material and helps coming from the General Department.

Music

1. **What is the place of music in a C.M.E. Church?**

Music is most prominent as part of the public worship of the people of God. In giving instructions to the Pastor as leader of worship the *Discipline* directs as follows: "It is urged that the Minister earnestly request all of the people to join in the Public Worship of God; first, by singing; ..."[5] And of the components used in the Service in which the Sacraments are administered singing is one of the three that may not be omitted. Prayer and the apostolic benediction are the other two.

While singing is not the only kind of "music" it is the one common to all of our churches. And being vocal it lends itself to the inclusion of more people in the acts of worship.

2. **Who gives directions on music?**

Since music is part of what is done in the public worship of God and since the Pastor in the C.M.E.

Church is responsible for providing leadership in planning and executing acts of worship the Pastor is to provide the directions.

3. **Does this mean that the Pastor "dictates" everything that is done regarding music?**

By no means is that the case. Unfortunately, we are hasty in giving a negative meaning to such phrases as "in charge" or to such words as "leader". A pastor will counsel with others who are co-workers in the music ministry of the church. His or her role as pastor includes preaching, which means that the theme or that the themes of each worship service grow out of the sermon. So the music, hymns and songs,as far as possible, is organized around the sermon. Thus, when the Pastor is put up front in this matter, it should be seen in the larger context of worship and not in light of the Pastor as dictator.

4. **How is the Choirster or Director of Music chosen?**

The Pastor presents the name of a person who is a member of the C.M.E. Church to the Quarterly Conference which elects the person.

5. **How is a church organist hired or selected?**

The Pastor and Church Officers select an organist. But if they cannot agree on a person for the position, the Pastor has the last word and may make the selection.

Again, this process and procedure must be seen, if it is to be rightly understood, in light of who is responsible for worship services in a local church and in view of the place of instrumental music in corporate worship.

6. **What directions do we have regarding choirs in the Local Church?**

   Each church is to have a choir, as far as that is practicable. Each choir shall have a President who shall be elected by its members and presented by the Pastor to the Quarterly Conference for confirmation or rejection.

USHERS

1. **Who organizes the ushers in the Local Church?**

   If a local church does not have a board of ushers, it is incumbent upon the Pastor to take "the initiative" in organizing one.

   Why? Ushers are servants of the servants who come into the house of the Lord to worship Him. As the leader of worship a Pastor knows the importance of ushers to the orderly execution of a service of worship. Where there is not a board a Pastor, I believe, would see the need for one.

2. **Is it the duty of the Pastor to appoint the officers of the Usher Board?**

   No. The *Discipline* gives the authority to elect officers to the members of the Usher Board. The President shall be a member of the Quarterly Conference.[6]

3. **What are the duties of the ushers?**

   The duties are (a) to admit people to the house of the Lord; (b) to attend to their comfort while they are there, and (c) to perform other duties assigned them by the Pastor and the Official Board.

4. **Do we have any training that would cause our ushers in every place to perform in a near uniform way?**

We do not have a national training program for local church ushers. The National Convocation of the C.M.E. Church, the first of which was held in 1987, may serve as a type of forum for focusing attention on the need and an arena for providing basics to highlight need and how to meet it.

One available resource is the National Interdenominational Ushers Association. There are state groups that could provide information. A strong point in favor of this group is the fact they do not advocate violating the policies and practices of the various member denominations. The church's position is first.

WOMEN'S MISSIONARY SOCIETY

1. **How many societies may each local church have?**

There is to be only one Society. There may be several circles in the one Women's Missionary Society.

2. **How are the officers elected?**

They are elected by the Society members after a Nominations Committee presents a slate of officers. Nominations may be made from the floor.

The President must be presented by the Pastor for confirmation.

3. **What is the relationship of the Pastor to the Society?**

The Pastor is an ex-officio member, without a vote.

4. **Is the Society open to men?**
The Constitution of the Women's Missionary Council states regarding the Local Society: "Membership shall be open to any member of the Christian Methodist Episcopal Church who desires to participate in the mission of the Local Church through the Women's Missionary Society."[7]

5. **Where may I get more information on the Women's Missionary Council?**
You may get the information from the *Handbook of the WMC*, which may be purchased through the Council.

LAY MINISTRY

1. **Who are the personnel of the Local Church that are responsible for the program of Lay Activities?**
The Pastor, the Lay Leader and the Board of Stewards are responsible.

2. **Who makes up the Local Lay Board?**
The Pastor is ex-officio, all of the Officers of the Lay Council and "All Chairpersons of Boards, Departments, Circles and Clubs" make it up.[8]

3. **How is the organization of the Lay Council effected?**
After the session of the Annual Conference the Lay Leader in cooperation with the Pastor calls all of the lay members of the Pastoral Charge together for organization purposes.

4. **Is the Local Lay Council related to a Connectional group?**
Yes. The Connectional body is the General Department of Lay Ministry. That name was voted in 1986

by the General Conference. It had been known as the General Department of Lay Activities.

It is headed by a General Secretary who is elected by General Conference. And it is organized at the Annual and District Conference levels and functions under a Lay Leader at each level.

A GLOSSARY OF TERMS

ALTAR — A table in the furnishings of a church where the Holy Communion is administered. It is also known as the Communion Table. Some experts on the subject say that the location determines whether it is called an Altar or Communion Table. If it is against a wall it is proper to call it the Altar. Other scholars do not seem to follow that line of thought.

ALTAR CROSS — A metal or wood cross that stands on the altar. Other objects placed on the altar, candles or flowers, should not stand higher than the cross.

BAPTISM — One of two sacraments, the other being Holy Communion. It is a sign of regeneration and of entry into the Church or the body of Christ.

BAPTISMAL FONT — A basin, stone or metal, for holding baptismal water.

BENEDICTION — The pronouncement of God's blessing and comes usually at the end of a service of worship.

CANDELABRA — Three, five, or seven branched holders in which candles are placed.

CATHOLIC — The term means universal and when used with Church it designates the universal fellowship of the people of God. It is used in the lower case or with a small "c" when used as "holy catholic church".

CHALICE — It is the cup used in the administration of Holy Communion.

CHANCEL — The chancel is the area in a church that is elevated above the nave and is divided by the CHANCEL RAIL. The area includes pulpit and choir loft or stand.

CHANCEL RAIL — In our churches we call it the Altar. But it is traditionally the divider between the NAVE, which is the area where worshippers sit, and the CHANCEL. In classically designed church buildings the area beyond the CHANCEL is the SANCTUARY which is the area where the ALTAR is situated and it is the highest area in the church. No matter which geographical end it is place, the ALTAR is always the East End.

COLLECT — A short prayer designed for use on special occasions.

CREED — A short concise and generally a minimal statement of faith or beliefs which worshippers use to state their belief.

CROSS — It is the universal symbol of our Lord's death. It is designed without Jesus hanging on it.

DOXOLOGY — A response often used at the close of a service.

EPISTLE SIDE — The right side of the church facing the ALTAR. It is the side on which the lectern for reading the Epistle stands.

GLORIA PATRI — Latin for "Glory be to the Father." It is a response sung after scripture reading or a creed.

GOSPEL SIDE — The left side facing the ALTAR is the Gospel or preaching side, when there are two stands.

HOST — The bread or wafer used in the sacrament of Holy Communion.

INDEX — The common and abbreviated way of referring to the official organ of the C.M.E. Church, *The Christian Index.*

INTROIT — A scripture that is said or sung at the opening of a service of worship.

LAVABO — A small bowl used to put water for cleansing the fingers.

LITURGICAL COLORS — There are five colors: white, red, violet, green, and black. *White* symbolizes purity and light. *Red* symbolizes blood, fire, and christian zeal. *Violet* or *purple* symbolizes penitence and fasting. *Green* symbolizes hope. *Black* symbolizes mourning.

NARTHEX — The portion of the church where the congregation enters. It is the western end and is sometimes called the vestibule.

NAVE — The portion of the church where the congregation sits.

OFFERING — The worshippers response through the giving of their possessions for the blessing of God and for His earthly work.

ORDINATION — The act of setting apart a preacher for some particular priestly and pastoral functions. Annual conferences elect preachers for orders and bishops ordain.

PASTOR — One who is a shepherd.

SANCTUARY — It commonly refers to the whole area in which people worship. Technically, it is the area in which the ALTAR is situated.

VESTMENTS — Garments worn by the clergy, acolytes, and choir members are called vestments. They should hide rather than call attention to the individ uals. Certain colors of vestments especially *red-purple* is reserved for bishops.

WINE — The fruit of the vine, and is one of the two elements used in the sacrament of Holy Communion, the other element being bread or wafer.

WORSHIP — The total response of human beings to the worth-ship of God, who is declared worthy to be praised because of having experienced His love, goodness, and mercy.

YEAR — The Christian Church Year begins with *Advent* which means coming of Christ and is the Sunday nearest November 30. Advent consists of four Sundays prior to Christmas. The color used is purple or violet.

Christmastide runs from Christmas Day through January 5th. The color is white.

Epiphany Season runs from Epiphany (to show), January 6th and runs for a variable number of Sundays. The date of Easter determines the length of Epiphany. The color is green.

Lent. This season begins on Ash Wednesday which is 40 days before Easter not counting the Sundays. The color is purple or violet.

Easter. The Easter season begins on Easter eve. It runs for 50 days, ending on the eve of Pentecost. Easter is the first Sunday after the first full moon falling upon or after March 21, which is the first day of Spring. In case the full moon comes on Sunday, Easter is the next Sunday. The period when Easter can place is between March 22 and April 25. The color for Easter is white.

Ascension Day is forty days after Easter and is on a Thursday. It is the day the Christ ascended into heaven. The color is white.

Pentecost is fifty days after Easter. It is the day when the Holy Ghost came upon the disciples in the upper room in Jerusalem. The color is red.

NOTES

CHAPTER II

[1]A. A. Benton, ed. *The Church Cyclopedia* (Philadelphia, L. R. Hamersly and Co., 1884), p. 74

[2]Ibid.

[3]Ibid., p. 75

[4]*Discipline*, 1986, Item 8, p. 28

[5]Ibid, Par. 210, Item 1, p. 41

[6]Jack M. Tuell, *The Organization of the United Methodist Church*. Nashville, Abingdon, 1970), p. 27.

[7]Ibid., p. 27f.

[8]Ibid.

[9]*Discipline*, 1986, Article 2, P. 165

[10]Ibid., p. 28

[11]Ibid., p. 15

[12]Benton, op. cit., p. 354

[13]*Discipline*, 1966, p. 174

[14]Ibid., pp. 16-17

[15]Ibid., par. 126, p. 16

[16]Ibid., par. 129, p. 17

[17]Ibid.

[18]John Wesley, *The Works of*, Vol. 10 (Baker Book House Grand Rapids, MI, 1984) p. 90f.

[19]*Discipline*, 1966, p. 29, Item 4

[20]Ibid., p. 31, Amendments, Article 2

[21]Ibid., par. 127, p. 17

[22]Ibid., par. 126, p. 16

[23]Ibid., p. 26, Article 5

[24]Ibid., p. 67, Question 3

[25]W. E. Vine, *An Expository Dictionary Of New Testament Words* (Fleming H. Revell Co., Westwood, N.J., 1966) p. 242.

[26]Fredrick A. Norwood, *The Story of American Methodism* (Abingdon, Nashville, 1981) p. 51

[27]Ibid.

[28]Wesley, op. cit., Vol. 5, p. 446

[29]Ibid.

[30]Ibid., p. 110f.

[31]Ibid., Vol. 8, p. 269

[32]*Discipline*, pars. 130-130:3, pp. 18-22

[33]Ibid., par. 130:2, p. 19

[34]*A Plain Account of Christian Perfection* (Beacon Hill Press, Kansas City, MO, 1966) p. 11

[35]*Works*, Vol. 10, p. 90

[36]Ibid., Vol. 6, p. 354

[37]Perkins School of Theology *Journal*, Spring 1984, See "John Wesley's Spiritual Disciplines For Today" by Bert Afleck, p. 2, and "Wesleyan Constructive Theology" by Charles M. Wood, p. 15

[38]One part of the Resolution of the General Conference Committee On Church Organization, Quoted in *Basic Christian Methodist Beliefs*, Bishop Joseph A. Johnson, Jr. (4th Episcopal District Press, Shreveport, LA, 1978) p. 14

[39]Norwood, op. cit., p. 125

[40]William J. Henry and William L. Harris, *Ecclesiastical Law* (September 1, 1878) p. 26 (Written as an interpretation of law in the M.E. Church)

[41]*Discipline*, 1986, par. 901, p. 165

[42]Wesley's *Works*, Vol.1, p. 103

[43]Gerald F. Kennedy, *The Methodist Way Of Life* (Prentice-Hall, Inc., Englewood Cliffs, N.J., 1958) p. 14f.

[44]Milton H. Borens, Sr., "John Wesley, The Father of Methodism". A study brochure published, 8th District, 1972, Norris S. Curry, Bishop .

[45]Quoted from *Wesley's Journal*, Vol. 2, p. 353, by Oscar Sherwin in *John Wesley Friend Of The People* (Twaye Publishers, N.Y., 1961) p. 66

[46]Fredrick A. Norwood. *The Story Of American Methodism* (Abingdon, Nashville, 1974) pp. 65-76

[47]Gerald F. Moede, *The Office Of Bishop In Methodism* (Abingdon, N.Y., 1964) p. 49

[48]Norwood, Ibid., p. 127

[49]Kennedy, Ibid., p. 84f.

[50]Othal H. Lakey, *The History Of The C.M.E. Church* (C.M.E. Publishing House, Memphis, 1985) p. 91f.

[51]William J. Walls, *The A.M.E. Zion Church* (A.M.E. Zion Publishing House, Charlotte, N.C., 1974) p. 83

[52]Norwood, p. 174

CHAPTER III

[1]Bishop Norris Curry, *The Methodist Preacher. Prophet, Priest And Pastor* (M.C. Curry, Los Angeles, 1977) contains a statement on the Trinity that author became acquainted with from reading literature of the M.E. Church, South. In part it states. ''That is we say that God the Father plans, God the Son executes, and God the Holy Spirit applies,'' p. 7.

[2]J. Oswald Sanders, *The Holy Spirit and His Gifts* (Zondervan, Grand Rapids, MI, 1970) p. 61ff.

[3]Ibid., Chapter 7

[4]Wesley, *Works*, Vol. 5, pp. 37-38

[5]Lawrence Boadt, *Reading The Old Testament* (Paulist Press, New York City, 1984) p. 11

[6]George Potts, *Background To the Bible*, (Harper and Row, N.Y., 1966) O.T. books, p. 23

[7]Suzanne deDietrich, *Discovering the Holy Bible*, (Source Publishers, Nashville 1953), p. 7

[8]*Discipline*, 1986, Article of Religion 6, p. 10

[9]Ibid., Article 5, p. 10

[10]George Potts, Background To the Bible (Harper and Row, N.Y., 1966) O.T. books, p. 111, N.T. 47f.

[11]*Discipline*, p. 10f.
[12]Ibid., Article 12, p. 12
[13]Charles W. Carter, *Contemporary Wesleyan Theology*, Vol. 1., Gen. Ed. Francis Asbury Press, Grand Rapids, MI, 1983) p. 86
[14]Wesley *Works*, Vol. 5, p. 224
[15]Ibid., p. 225
[16]Op. cit.
[17]Ibid., p. 228
[18]Ibid., p. 230
[19]Op. cit. (The emphasis is mine.)
[20]Ibid., p. 232
[21]*Discipline*, Par. 128, p. 17
[22]Wesley's *Works*, Vol. 5, p. 233
[23]*Discipline*, Ibid.
[24]*New Testament In Basic English*
[25]*The Cambridge Bible Commentary* (Gospel According To Matthew) p. 96
[26]W. E. Vine, *Expository Dictionary Of New Testament Words* (Revell Co., Westwood, N.J., 1966) p. 316
[27]Ibid., op. cit.
[28]Wesley's *Works*, Vol. 1, p. 160
[29]Ibid.
[30]Wesley, Vol. 8, p. 371
[31]*Works*, Vol. 12, p. 60
[32]*Discipline*, Par. 110, Art. 10, P. 11
[33]*Works*, Vol. 7, pp. 256-264
[34]Ibid., p. 263
[35]Ibid., p. 261
[36]*Works*, Vol. 12, p. 399
[37]Vine, op. cit., p. 284
[38]*Works*, Vol. 5, p. 223f.
[39]Vine, op. cit., p. 267
[40]Ibid., p. 238
[41]*Conversion* (Muhlenberg Press, Philadelphia, 1960) p. 1
[42]Vine, op. cit., p. 280

[43]Routley, op. cit., p. 4
[44]*A Plain Account Of Christian Perfection*, p. 41
[45]Ibid., p. 42
[46]Ibid., p. 43
[47]From *Wesley's Journal*, Feb. 21, 1771 and quoted in *The Methodist First Reader* by Charles C. Selecman and George H. Jones, Methodist Evangelistic Material, Nashville, 1958) p. 53
[48]John C. Irwin, *On Being A Christian* (Abingdon, Nashville, 1958) p. 15
[49]Selecman and Jones, op. cit., p. 33
[50]Quoted by Selecman and Jones, op. cit., p. 59

CHAPTER IV

[1]Addison H. Leitch, *Interpreting Basic Theology* (Hawthorn Books, N.Y., 1961) p. 165
[2]*Discipline*, p. 13
[3]D. M. Baillie, *The Theology of the Sacraments* (Charles Scribner's Sons, New York, 1957) p. 55
[4]Quoted from ''New Testament Reading Guide,'' No. 13, Liturgical Press (Collegeville, MN, 1965) in *The Sacraments: An Experiment In Ecumenical Honesty* (Abingdon, Nashville, 1969) p. 27f.
[5]Baillie, op. cit., p. 53
[6]Ibid.
[7]Fiedler and Garrison, p. 35
[8]Baillie, op. cit., p. 85
[9]Charles W. Carter, ed., *A Contemporary Wesleyan Theology*, Vol. 2 (Francis Asbury Press, Grand Rapids, MI, 1983) p. 616
[10]*Wesley's Works*, Vol. 8, p. 48
[11]*Discipline*, Art. 17, p. 13
[12]Carter, Op. cit , Vol. 2

[13]Martin E. Marty, *Baptism* (Muhlenberg, Philadelphia, 1962) p. 16

[14]J. S. Whale, *Christian Doctrine* (Cambridge 1956) p. 160

[15]Fiedler and Garrison, p. 43f.

[16]Ibid.

[17]*Works*, Vol. 10, p. 188

[18]*Works*, Vol. 6, p. 74

[19]*The Sacraments*, p. 36

[20]*Christian Doctrine*, p. 165f.

[21]*Works*, Vol. 10, p. 193

[22]Ibid, Vol. 6, p. 68

[23]Op. cit., p. 193

[24]*One Baptism, One Eucharist, And A Mutually Recognized Ministry* (W.C.C., 1975) p. 16

[25]*Baptism, Eucharist and Ministry* (W.C.C., 1982) p. 7

[26]Op. cit., p. 13

[27]Whale, p. 163

[28]*Works*, Vol. 10, p. 191

[29]John A. T. Robinson, *Liturgy Coming To Life* (Westminster, Philadelphia, 1963) p. 53

[30]*Discipline*, Pars. 118, 119, p. 13f

[31]Baillie, p. 98

[32]Jurgen Moltmann, *Experiences of God*, (Fortress, Philadelphia, 1980) p. 33

[33]*Discipline*, 1986, Par. 113, Article 13, p. 12

[34]Ibid., ''Preamble'', p. 25

[35]Op. cit., Article 1

[36]Ibid., p. 19

[37]*Discipline*, ''Sex and Human Life'', p. 22

[38]Op. cit., Read the ''Theological Perspective'' of the Social Creed, p. 18f. and sections (e) and (f) on page 22

[39]*Human Life A Biblical Perspective For Bioethics* (Fortress Press, Philadelphia, 1984) p. 66

[40]Op. cit., p. 66

[41]Ibid., p. 66

[42]T. A. Kantonen, *Life After Death* (Muhlenberg Press, Philadelphia, 1962) p. 9

[43]Op. cit.

[44]Nelson, op. cit., p. 89

[45]*Life AfterDeath*, p.11

[46]Rogert Shinn, *Life, Death and Destiny* (Westminster, Philadelphia, 1957)

[47]Kantonen, op cit., p. 15

[48]Nelson, op. cit., p. 70

[49]Kantonen, p. 9

[50]Nelson, p. 70

[51]Quoted by Kantonen, p. 8

[52]Ibid., p. 9

[53]Merrill R. Abbey, *Creed Of Our Hope* (Abingdon, Nashville, 1954) p. 106.

[54]Oscar Cullmann, *Immortality of the Soul or Resurrection of the Dead?* (Epworth Press, London, 1958) p. 38

[55]Ibid., p. 55

[56]Ibid., p. 27

[57]Cullman, p. 17ff.

[58]Nelson, op. cit., p. 91

[59]Kantonen, p. 29

[60]Oscar Cullmann, *Christ and Time* (Westminster Philadelphia 1954) p. 238

[61]Karl Heim, See: *The World. Its Creation and Consummation* (Muhlenberg Press, Philadelphia, 1962) p. 248.

[62]Kantonen, op. cit., p. 43

[63]Cullmann, *Christ and Time*, p. 236

[64]Abbey, *Creed Of Our Hope*, p. 104ff.

[65]Cullmann, *Immortality or the Resurrection, etc.*, p. 48

[66]Kantonen, op. cit., p. 34f.

[67]See.. Cullmann, *Immortality etc.*, Chapter 4

[68]Heim, op. cit., p. 149

[69]Shinn, op. cit., p. 77

[70]Georgia Harkness, *Beliefs That Count* (Abingdon, Nashville, 1961) p. 112
[71]Ibid., p. 114
[72]Shinn, op. cit., p. 87
[73]Kantonen, op. cit., 52

CHAPTER V

[1]Othal Hawthorne Lakey, *The History Of The C.M.E. Church* (C.M.E. Publishing House, Memphis, 1985) pp. 194-198
[2]Ibid., p. 197
[3]C. H. Phillips, *History Of The Colored M.E. Church* (Publishing House of The C.M.E. Church, Jackson, Tennessee, 1925) p. 39 (It is important to note that according to Phillips' reference to the third day as December 19 means that he too considered December 16 as the first day, provided each day was regarded as twenty four hours and the Conference looked upon as continuous days.)
[4]Lakey, op. cit., pp. 198-205
[5]Phillips, p. 36
[6]Lakey, p. 202
[7]*Discipline*, 1986, Amendments, Article 2, p. 31
[8]Ibid., Article 3, p. 31
[9]*Discipline*, Divisions 2, 3, 4, pp. 27-31
[10]Ibid., Div. 3, Episcopacy, Article 3, p. 30f.
[11]Ibid., 10th, p. 34
[12]*Minutes*, 24th Episcopal Meeting, May 1894, page 2 (typed copy)
[13]See: Lakey, p. 499, p. 521
[14]Nolan B. Harmon, *The Organization Of The Methodist Church*, 2nd Edition (The Methodist Publishing House, Nashville 1962) p. 98. The general information

presented was also influenced by Bishop Harmon, et. al.

[15]Gerald Moede, *The Office Of Bishop In Methodism* (Publishing House of the Methodist Church, Zurich, Switzerland, 1964) p. 17

[16]*Discipline*, Par. 201.2, p. 38

[17]Ibid., Par. 201.1

[18]Harmon, op. cit, p. 98

[19]*Discipline*, Par. 202, p. 39

[20]Ibid., Par. 204, p. 40

[21]Ibid., Constitution, Sect. 2, Article 2, p. 27f.

[22]Ibid., Par. 212, p. 42

[23]Ibid., Par. 520.1, p. 100f.

[24]Harmon, Ibid., p. 148 (See the mandating as set out in the Discipline, Par. 244, p. 63).

[25]*Discipline*, Par. 244.1, p. 63

[26]Ibid., Div. Two, Art. 5, p. 27

[27]Ibid., Par. 249, p. 69

[28]Harmon, Ibid., p. 161

[29]Ibid.

[30]*Discipline*, Par. 249, p. 69

[31]Ibid., Par. 216, p. 42f.

[32]Ibid., Par. 256, p. 71

[33]Harmon, op. cit. p. 157f.

[34]*Discipline*, p. 29

[35]Ibid., ''Appeals'' p. 166

[36]Ibid., ''Declaratory Decisions'' #1, p. 166

[37]Lakey, op. cit., p. 525

CHAPTER VI

[1]*Discipline*, Par. 522, #1, p. 105

[2]*Discipline*, Par. 1223.3, p. 257

[3]Ibid., Par. 1223.9, p. 257

[4]Ibid., Par. 1256.1, p. 281
[5]Ibid., Par. 401, No. 4, p. 81
[6]Ibid., Par. 614, No. 2, p. 137
[7]Ibid., Par. 1234, Section 14, p. 269
[8]Ibid., Par. 1239.2, p. 278